AT
ENJOYING
THE FREEDOM
YOU FOUGHT FOR
EASE.

A Soldier's Story and Perspectives on the
Journey to an Encore Life and Career

PRAISE FOR
AT EASE: ENJOYING THE FREEDOM YOU FOUGHT FOR

"Detailed planning, preparation, and execution are key to success on any military operation. *At Ease* is a practical, inspirational, fun, must-read book that will help reduce the challenges one faces in planning and preparing for *operation transition*. Rob Campbell's transparent and humble character shines through in this gift to our proud brothers and sisters in uniform."

Lawson W. Magruder, III
Lieutenant General, U.S. Army Retired
President, LWMIII Consulting, LLC
True Growth Leadership

"A wonderful and useful read. This is a one-of-a-kind book to inform and guide a servicemember through a profound change in their life. The Defense Department ought to make this standard issue for transitioning veterans!"

James T. Hill
General, U.S. Army Retired

"A must-read for all who transition from the military to civilian life. Transition is an eye-opener and a reality that every military service member will eventually face. This book will bring that into perspective to help all understand what to expect when transitioning from the hardest *career* in their life to the hardest *change* in their life."

Nathan Aguinaga
Master Sergeant, U.S. Army Retired

Author of *Division: Life on Ardennes Street* and *Roster Number Five-Zero*

"Rob hit a grand slam with this powerful book for senior leaders transitioning out of the military. For those of us in denial that this day would ever come, Rob vividly describes his story so that the reader can learn the good, bad and ugly of his journey. He teaches us to embrace a journey that culminates with a life and post-military career filled with love, family, meaning, passion and fulfillment — a life you earned and deserve. Every senior leader exiting our military should read this book and pay forward their lessons learned. Well done, Rob!"

Adam Rocke
Colonel, U.S. Army Retired

Senior Director, U.S. Chamber of Commerce, Hiring Our Heroes Foundation

"Rob Campbell has written a book unlike any other. It clearly captures the lessons encountered hiking through the peaks and valleys of the transition process, while revealing the importance of asking critical questions that can ensure your values-driven military life translates into a fulfilling, values-driven civilian life. It is a must-read primer for every servicemember considering transition."

Scott "Topper" Farr
Captain, U.S. Navy Retired

"Rob Campbell has wisdom, intelligence, and experience. However, more importantly, he has the resolve to pass these attributes — and the lessons he learned along the way — to others so they may benefit from his hard work and sacrifice. In his first book, *It's Personal, Not Personnel: Leadership Lessons for the Battlefield and the Boardroom*, Rob explained how he and his organizations achieved so much success in war and peace. Now he has tackled an even more daunting task in *At Ease*. How do you take care of yourself when this is all over? This book should be in every Soldier for Life Center in the U.S. Army and required reading for all those who are leaving the military regardless if you did 3 or 30."

Kenneth E. Wolfe
Command Sergeant Major, U.S. Army Retired
Director of Operations, Tough Stump Technologies

"Transition is not a one-time activity, a period of time or a phase. Instead, Rob recognizes that it is a continuous journey. No matter how successful your military career may have been, you need more than resume tips, job prospects and a fancy title. This book will push you to think and act more deeply, ultimately leading to greater fulfillment and living at your potential in an encore career."

Pete Marston
Former Army Captain
Project Director, Veteran Leader, Transition Program Founder

"*At Ease* is groundbreaking literature for the post-9/11 generation, the 'Learning to Eat Soup with a Knife' kind of guide to life after the military. Veterans and civilians alike can blaze a new path after reading this book."

Marjorie K. Eastman
Former Army Captain and Military Spouse
Award-Winning author of *The Frontline Generation*

"The decision to leave the military, especially after having dedicated one's adult life to it, is highly emotional and personal. COL Rob Campbell uses his experience to help others prepare for and navigate what is a life-changing event. By sharing the emotional ups and downs, the second guessing, the "Is it time?" discussions with his wife, Leslie, and their kids, he allows others to peek behind the curtain and he provides incredibly relevant things to consider. *At Ease* is a great resource for anyone contemplating their ETS, whether it's after a three-year initial assignment or after a 30-year career."

William J. Butler, Colonel
U.S. Army Retired
Chief of Staff
National Veterans Memorial and Museum

"Stop your research for books on transitioning out of the military. *At Ease* gets to the heart of the matter. Rob shares details of his life ... family triumphs and struggles. It's inspirational and you will easily identify ... as if he were writing about your career and life. You have more than earned the right to an abundant second career and exciting life. Read this book now to find out how to make your transition an exceptional experience."

Scott Campbell
Colonel, U.S. Air Force Retired
Mentor ... Encourager ... Helping Others Succeed

Marva Campbell
Military Spouse

"Through the lens of his own journey, Rob Campbell captures and normalizes the emotions we feel when considering leaving the military: fear, guilt, excitement and empowerment. He reassures us that, while the process is not easy, we are not alone. *At Ease* isn't a how-to book of transition checklists and timelines. It's a raw look into the ups and downs of leaving the service, and a guidebook on how to discover and define what fulfillment means to you in the next phase of life. This book is a refreshing reminder that we can find purpose and passion in this second phase of life. It's a must-have for those about to separate or retire, as well as recently transitioned veterans, whether you served for 10 years or 30."

Tim Kuppler
Former Army Captain
Director of Digital Marketing

"If you've decided to leave the military, you must read this book. Rob Campbell masterfully combines pragmatic decisions about what's next professionally and personally, the emotion of leaving the tribe and its warrior culture, and dealing with the, 'you don't know what you don't know' that awaits us all when we take off the uniform. There are many transition books out there, but this one takes you on a unique ride — and lets you see the journey through the eyes and emotion of someone with as distinguished a career as anyone who's been down the transition road. *At Ease* is an enjoyable story and an invaluable handrail for anyone leaving military service."

John Panaccione
Former Army Captain
CEO, LogicBay
Co-Founder VetToCEO

"I've observed Rob Campbell's inspiring leadership for nearly 20 years. Now he continues to serve — this time through his relevant and useful story and perspectives on his journey to a fulfilling post-military life and career. A must-read for those on the cusp of transition."

Lieutenant General Michael Ferriter
U.S. Army Retired
President and CEO
National Veterans Memorial and Museum

"Having commanded 5,000 military personnel in one of the most hostile environments on the planet, Rob Campbell could be forgiven for thinking he had 'work/life' figured out. He'd spent 27 years being saluted, often by people he had never met. What else was there to learn? Surely he thought transition would be a walk in the park for a combat veteran? Not a chance. With refreshing humility, Rob makes his experiences instructive for us all, guiding readers as they tread their own, authentic paths. If you want your encore career to be about purpose and passion, rather than just paychecks and job titles, this book is for you!"

Jim Hughes
Founder of Untamed Entrepreneurs
Know Yourself. Find Your Playground.

"Transitioning from the military is hard. It's hard on the troop, it's hard on the family and it lies in the realm of the unknown. I loved how Colonel Rob Campbell attacked this topic through vulnerability, reality, and phenomenal storytelling. Everyone and their brother will tell you how to write a resume, or that it's your network that counts … but what all of us want when transitioning is to hear from others who have gone before us. And now we have the book on it and it's a must-read! Great job, Rob. I salute you for your continuing dedication and commitment to leading the troops. Hooah!"

Robert "Bo" Brabo
Chief Warrant Officer 3, U.S. Army Retired
Author of *From the Battlefield to the White House to the Boardroom*

"Rob devotes significant time and energy to aiding veterans during the transition journey. His optimism compels all of us to seek strength and courage, especially in the most challenging times. His servant leadership approach to the veteran population is unmatched."

Warren Lanigan
Former Army Captain

"Colonel Rob Campbell has accumulated an invaluable set of knowledge, experience and wisdom during his 27 years in the United States Army. As Brigade Commander, he was responsible for 5,000 combat-ready war fighters. He excelled at it. Phase two of Rob's journey would add additional tools to his already overflowing toolbox. He coaches and mentors other leaders, delivers keynote speeches and he's written multiple, successful books. He's an entre-preneur with his own business. Rob gets it. He understands the transition our service members experience when leaving the unique culture of the wartime military — and then entering an almost equally unique and bizarre culture of society in 2020 and beyond. A great book for the transitioning warrior. Thank you, Rob!"

Monty Heath
Special Warfare Operator, 1st Class, U.S. Navy SEAL

"For those of us entering transition from the military, the leap into the unknown generates a strong urge to grab ahold of 'top-down' guidance. What industries are hiring? Which head hunters might find us attractive? How do I mold my resume to fit into these immediately visible openings? In *At Ease*, Rob Campbell takes a longer view and a 'bottom-up' approach. The book chapters become a wonderful exer-cise in reflecting on the principles and life values that came to define our military careers, family lives, and who we are as individuals. From this framework, Rob arms transitioning military members to identify core principles for our post-military lives. From this, we can look beyond just getting that first job. And instead we can truly think about and work toward building an encore career and next chapter in life as rewarding and meaningful as our first career in the military."

Bill Raskin
Lieutenant Colonel, U.S. Army Retired
First Career: Army Special Forces Officer
Second Career: Writer and Consultant
Author of the Debut Novel, *Cardiac Gap*

"Transitioning from active duty service to the civilian world is more intimidating and anxiety-ridden than many would like to admit. However, Rob masterfully shares through this new book how any servicemember can embrace their next mission. I highly recommend reading *At Ease* for anyone going through this transition."

Siobhan R. Norris
U.S. Army Veteran (Specialist) and Military Spouse
Program Manager, Military and Veterans Affairs
The University of North Carolina System Office

"*At Ease* is a guide for you and your family as you start the journey from a lifetime in the military to the rest of your life. This book was incredibly helpful to us as we sought to find balance and direction and to start making critical decisions as we prepared to retire. Rob and Leslie took us along on their journey from thinking about retiring, to retiring, and then the new reality after the military. They offered great insights we needed for our own journey. As you face this important decision, let Rob and Leslie help you recognize the incredible opportunities ahead and enjoy your incredible successes serving our Country."

Brian Scott
Lieutenant Colonel, U.S. Army Retired
Vice President
Nisqually Reach Nature Center

Suzanne Scott
Colonel, U.S. Army Retired
Chief Nursing Officer
Providence, Southwest Washington

AT EASE.

ENJOYING THE FREEDOM YOU FOUGHT FOR

A Soldier's Story and Perspectives on the Journey to an Encore Life and Career

Colonel Rob Campbell

UNITED STATES ARMY, RETIRED

SILVER TREE PUBLISHING

DEDICATION

To Leslie, Robbie, Meggie and Louden.

And to all the servicemembers who gave their lives in service to their nation so that we can enjoy our encore life. May we honor them by living good lives.

TABLE OF CONTENTS

PART TWO
Perspectives and Philosophies

PART THREE
Parting Thoughts and Resources

INTRODUCTION

There I was. Late October of 2015, Colorado Springs, Colorado ...
a beautiful part of the country and a place my family and I had always
wanted to be stationed. It took us 26 years to get there. *Whew, we
made it!* We were happy to have arrived in such a great place and
were eager to take in all its riches. This assignment for me, number
14, would turn out to be my last — *our* last. Life *after* the Army lay
before me ... an end and a beginning. But I didn't know it yet.

I had just finished commanding the 1st Brigade of the 101st Airborne
Division, which included a deployment to Afghanistan. Shortly after
my return from combat, I sent my wife, Leslie, and our youngest son,
Louden, off to Colorado Springs a full three months ahead of me so
Louden could start high school on time for his senior year. Needless
to say, it was a few years of high adventure for the Campbells and, at
long last, we were once again together, a treasure we cherished most
through a career of both brief and extended separations.

I was a Colonel entering the post-command phase of my career —
new territory, for sure, because this phase, unlike the others, might
come with an abrupt end. We found ourselves on post again, this
time on an Air Force Base named Peterson. I was assigned to run the
operations center for U.S. Northern Command (NORTHCOM). There
was something more to this assignment though. It would be our last.

It was never the "grand plan" to convince the Army to post us in Colorado, then pull the plug on my military career. When I took time to reflect upon it, I guess I never really had a plan at all. Like many, I just worked hard and the Army rewarded me with some great assignments serving alongside people I remain close with today. Nevertheless, here we were in NORTHCOM, facing a relatively calm two years void of combat, where we could catch our breath, enjoy some much-needed family time and ponder our future. To this point in my career I had followed the Army's traditional path of assignments and promotions, moving up in rank and responsibility in tactical (or what we called "muddy boots" assignments), achieving the rank of Colonel and the responsibility of brigade command. Now, on the other side of that somewhat predictable progression, with clean boots, never to serve in a brigade again, I faced the next chapter of my career, competing to be a general officer and taking off on a much less predictable path. As it would turn out, I would submit my retirement instead, and my family and I would begin a journey out of the military and into civilian life.

THE DECISION TO RETIRE

· ·

"I'm going to retire from the military" is simple to say or write in a sentence, but enormous in its practicalities and long-term implications.

· ·

The decision to retire was not an easy one. Indeed, the decision was a journey in and of itself. Once made, it would be step one of a path I am still traveling. Of course, the decision would be the most important part ... requiring deep thought and conversation with family, friends and mentors. It would set in motion a huge transition from soldier to civilian, active duty servicemember to retiree.

"I'm going to retire from the military" is simple to say or write in a sentence, but enormous in its practicalities and long-term implications. I would have to learn how to do that — how to bid the military a fond farewell, something I had never considered. I would have to learn to do a lot of things I had never done and experience things I had not imagined. It felt wonderful and frightening all at the same time. I was enlightened and disappointed all at once. There were highs and lows (and there still are). The space I was about to step into was vast and unexplored, at least by me. I had 1,000 big ideas, if not "great ideas," and still do. Most of all, I wanted to take what I had earned and learned in the military create a new life of fulfillment. Not a job, but a whole *life*. I viewed the future as a blank sheet of paper, where I could write a new story. I wanted to enjoy the freedom I had fought for.

. . . .

I wanted to enjoy the freedom I had fought for. I want that for you too.

. . . .

I want that for you too. Welcome to my book. In the stories and perspectives I share, you'll not only bear witness to the open pages of my journey from servicemember to civilian, but you'll also have the opportunity to consider the "open pages" of your own current or future military/civilian transition. I will share my story of transition, tell you what I learned along the way, and provide you with philosophies to consider in your decision and journey. I'll take you through the difficulty of making a decision I had to "reprogram myself" to make. You'll experience the angst, frustration, freedom, nervousness, doubt, resentment and bliss I experienced through the transition out of the Army and into a civilian life — back into a life I had left behind, decades ago and which had changed in many ways.

Chapter by chapter, I'll arm you with philosophies on how to approach each milestone and apply it to your own journey. I'll challenge traditional thinking, focusing instead on the pursuit of your true passion. I'll challenge you to be creative in your thinking about *lifestyle* over job. You'll be with me as I re-enter society, surrounded with people who speak "C-Suite, valuation and net worth" instead of "PCS, promotion board or mission command." My ego pays a visit more than once during the transition, showing you how difficult it was for me to exist in a society full of people who had no earthly idea what I had experienced or how much responsibility I once had in the Army. I'll talk about jobs, networking, your spouse, physical fitness and even downsizing your house and your stuff. I'll show you how your encore life and career can be thoroughly enjoyable.

· ·

Your encore life and career can be thoroughly enjoyable.

· ·

NOT JUST A JOB CHANGE OR A BIG CAREER MOVE: A TRUE TRANSITION IN LIFE

Most people reading this book have served in the Armed Forces for 10 years or more, which puts you sometime at a unique advantage in life but also puts you at a far remove from the civilian world you chose to exit for a period of time. Transitioning after more than a decade of service, amidst all its challenges, sets you apart from most people. It gives you options others don't have, and it can and should be a wonderful adventure.

This is not to say that you've arrived at Easy Street and can now buy a nice big rocking chair for the front porch. Retiring from the military is, for most of us, not a true retirement, but a transition into our next career. You see, our post-military fringe benefits (and even our pensions, if we stayed in long enough to earn them) will likely not provide the comforts we have become accustomed to. And, frankly, I don't subscribe to the notion of "we know how to live off of nothing." We don't want to live off of nothing, so we separate from the military and immediately set out to find our next mission. And missions, in the civilian world, are usually jobs.

Many of us, in our quest for money or in reaction to our fear of not being employed, will frantically reach for a lifeline and sprint toward a job. This uncreative rush to a paycheck and to a desk may violate our true passions in life, where we and our family want to live and how we want to embrace the new freedoms we now have. Moreover, it can result in a situation that goes far beyond the proverbial "more of the same" dilemma of jumping "out of the frying pan and into the fire." This rush to take any good-enough job that comes our way can thrust us into another high-pressure organization (albeit far different from the Army, Navy, Air Force, Marines or Coast Guard), sprinting up the corporate ladder at the speed of light.

. . . .

The uncreative rush to a paycheck and to a desk may violate our true passions in life, where we and our family want to live and how we want to embrace the new freedoms we now have.

. . . .

While most, including me, need a steady paycheck, we do have options. This book is written in the spirit of those options. It's written for those of us who have served during a particularly demanding time, much of it in the post-9/11 era dominated by two wars. It's written for those of us who have been institutionalized in a military career and life we loved, serving our nation and our men, women and their families. It's written for those of us who are about to enter or who have recently entered the post-military world. It's written for those of us willing to cast aside our egos, institutionalism and assumptions — those of us who want to challenge traditional paths and blaze our own.

WHAT'S IN THIS BOOK

Here is what you'll get and not get by reading *At Ease*. Though I will share tips and information about the steps I took or should have taken, I won't outline a rigid set of milestones you must achieve prior to departure. There are plenty of other great books out there with this approach, complete with exercises to prepare you for the next chapter in your life.

This is not a job-hunt book. While I will offer advice to help you look for fulfilling work, the pages ahead will not focus on the feverish hunt for a job. Again, there are plenty of books, webinars and seminars to help you. Instead I'll tell some stories. I'll open up about my struggles, then and now, living in this post-military life. I'll tell you what I got right and what I got wrong, and let you decide for yourself how you and your family should approach your own new world of wonder.

I'll introduce you to an unusual mentor of mine. I'll provide a few nuggets of research for your kit bag and I'll be honest, candid and sometimes crass. This post-military life is not a fairytale with unicorns, butterflies and sunny perfect days under the oak tree, napping with your trusty dog next to you (though I have done some of that, minus the unicorns). My recommendations and perspectives take real life into account. I won't suggest you jettison your obligations. I have a kid in college, cars and living expenses. I get it. You can and certainly will find moments of enchantment but, not far away, life will continue to rumble toward you, flowing back in to steal your personal nirvana.

Consider this book to be a "food for thought" snack to sustain you as you navigate your own river, following an amazing voyage serving our nation. Or look at it as ammunition or body armor to arm yourself for the next patrol. Whether you are a senior servicemember on the cusp of a planned departure from the military or one who is only beginning to think about the transition, this book is for you. Learn from my ups and downs. Take little pieces or consume the whole meal but go forward informed, authentically, with a creative, open mind and truly embrace what can be a life of fulfillment.

. . . .

How can your encore life and career be better than the last?

. . . .

Consider this question: How can your encore life and career be better than the last? We shouldn't live by the philosophy that our best days are behind us. What a terrible approach. Go chase something great. Are you ready? Pre-combat checks complete or shall I say — in civilian parlance — do you have your glasses, cell phone and wallet or purse? *Let's do this!*

TIMELINE

Wherever possible, the stories presented in this book endeavor to be clear about chronology, location and contexts. But, military life being what it is — with constantly changing posts, ranks, assignments and life circumstances — it's easy to get a little "lost" when bearing witness to someone else's life journey. So, for clarity and reference, I've provided a timeline here of my life and career, starting with the moment I first put on the uniform and taking you to where my life stands today.

Date	Milestone	Location
January 1987	Enlisted in the Army National Guard (as a college freshman)	Worchester, MA
October 1987	Joined ROTC	North Adams, MA
May 1990	Graduated college; Commissioned 2nd Lieutenant, Infantry	North Adams, MA
May 1991	Leslie and I married (high school sweethearts)	Townsend, MA
1990-1992	Infantry Officer's Basic Course, Ranger School	Fort Benning, GA
1992-1993	Platoon Leader, 199th Infantry Brigade	Fort Lewis, WA

Date	Milestone	Location
1993-1994	Troop Executive Officer, 2nd Cavalry Regiment	Fort Polk, LA
April 1994	First son, Robert (Robbie) Jr., is born	Fort Polk, LA
May 1994	Promotion to Captain	Fort Polk, LA
1994-1995	Infantry Officer's Advanced Course	Fort Benning, GA
1995-1999	Staff Officer, Company Commander, 25th Infantry Division	Schofield Barracks, HI
March 1998	Second son, Louden, is born	Honolulu, HI
1999-2002	General's Aide de Camp, I Corps	Fort Lewis, WA
April 2002	Promotion to Major	Fort Lewis, WA
2002-2003	Command General Staff College; Master's degree in administration (organizational behavior, structure, operations and personnel), Central Michigan University	Fort Leavenworth, KS
2003-2008	Operations and Executive Officer; 1st Combat Deployment — Iraq, 82nd Airborne	Fort Bragg, NC, and Tikrit, Iraq
2006	Promotion to Lieutenant Colonel	Tikrit, Iraq
2008-2010	Squadron Commander; 2nd Combat Deployment — Afghanistan, 25th Infantry Division	Fort Richardson, AK, and Gardez, Afghanistan
2008	Robbie begins high school	Anchorage, AK
2010-2012	Senior Combat Trainer	Hohenfels, Germany

Date	Milestone	Location
April 2012	Promotion to Colonel	Hohenfels, Germany
May 2012	Robbie graduates from high school	Hohenfels, Germany
2012	Louden begins high school	Mechanicsburg, PA
2012-2013	U.S. Army War College, Master's degree in strategic studies and defense	Carlisle Barracks, PA
2013-2015	Brigade Commander; 3rd Combat Deployment — Afghanistan, 101st Airborne Division	Fort Campbell, KY, and Kandahar, Afghanistan
2015-2016	Operations Officer, U.S. Northern Command	Peterson Air Force Base, CO
Fall/Winter 2015	Retirement discussions and decision to retire made; Army approval for retirement	Peterson Air Force Base, CO
May 2016	Louden graduates from high school	Colorado Springs, CO
August 2016	Final transition — Begin leave, move to the beach, close on a beach house	Fort Carson, CO, and Topsail Island, NC
September 2016-May 2017	Leslie takes a teaching position; Rob takes a year off to readjust and reflect	Wilmington, NC
September 2016	Hurricane Matthew	Topsail Island, NC
October 2016	Attended our 30th high school reunion	Massachusetts
October 2016	Retirement ceremony with friends and family	Washington, DC

Date	Milestone	Location
February-April 2017	Wrote my 1st book, *It's Personal, Not Personnel: Leadership Lessons for the Battlefield and the Boardroom*	Topsail Island, NC
May 2017	Started my business, Rob Campbell Leadership	Topsail Island, NC
May 2017	Leslie begins her art business	Topsail, Island, NC
October 2017	Published book #1	Topsail Island, NC
July 2017-April 2018	Adjunct Professor (part-time), U.S. Marine Corps Command and Staff College	Camp Lejeune, NC
November 2017	Almost jettisoned my business to take a financial advisor job	Jacksonville, NC
January 2018	First paying customer, Rob Campbell Leadership	Topsail Island, NC
March 2018	Took a job as a Vice President in a local company; this horrible experience lasted five days	Wilmington, NC
June 2018	Leslie and I were accepted to and attended a two-week artist/writer-in-residence program. Start of book #2, *At Ease: Enjoying the Freedom You Fought For*	Orquevaux, France
September 2018	Hurricane Florence; evacuated for two weeks	Topsail Island, NC
October 2018	Business begins to pick up	Wilmington, NC
November 2018	Thanksgiving in the mountains; more work on book #2	Asheville, NC
February 2019	Getting the itch to move and downsize	Topsail Island, NC

Date	Milestone	Location
March 2019	Sold our beach home and half of our unused belongings	Topsail Island, NC
April 2019	Moved into an urban apartment in downtown Wilmington, NC	Wilmington, NC
May 2019	Robbie and Meggie marry in Austria; family trip to Europe	Germany, Austria, Italy
July 2019	Trip to Alaska (business and pleasure)	Anchorage, AK
August 2019	Join Toastmasters International to grow as a professional speaker	Wilmington, NC
August 2019	Finished book #2	Asheville, NC
October 2019	Assume part-time duties as the Executive Director for VetToCEO, a nonprofit veteran entrepreneurship program	Wilmington, NC
October 2019	Leslie attends an Artist Residency in Bulgaria	Sofia, Bulgaria
October-November 2019	Joined Leslie in Bulgaria for her art show, then on to Germany to visit with Robbie and Meggie	Sofia, Bulgaria, and Vilsek, Germany
December 2019	Book #1 release in audiobook edition	Wilmington, NC
April 2020	Published book #2	Wilmington, NC

PART ONE
JOURNEY TO YOUR ENCORE LIFE

Chapter 1
STAY IN!

"What? Wait a minute ... I thought this was a book about the exit, about hanging up the uniform for the last time and stretching out my hammock for a peaceful nap with my new beard and ponytail. WTF, Campbell!" I know you're thinking it.

There's your first F-bomb (the book has at least a few ... just keeping it real, and I know you wouldn't expect anything less). But you probably *didn't* expect me to tell you to "stay in." OK, I do take a risk in beginning a transition book by telling you to stay in. What's the point of reading further, right? That's a fair assessment, but here's the thing. Now that I'm on the other side looking back, I believe it is an important start ... thinking about the military departure with a bit of skepticism and an open door to sticking it out. The point of this chapter is to remind you that the departure decision is yours to make. And just because you begin considering it doesn't mean you have to make the leap quickly or right then. It took me a year and a half from the first "should I stay or should I go?" conversations with my wife until the moment I hung up the uniform for the last time.

I'd like to start this book by highlighting all the great things we have as active servicemembers, to help you make an informed decision. I want to help you make an informed versus an emotional decision or what a mentor of mine once said, "avoid creating a permanent solution to a temporary problem." I almost did that. I want to help you decide "when."

MY FIRST MUSINGS ABOUT RETIRING FROM THE ARMY

I almost submitted my retirement as a Lieutenant Colonel, following command of a squadron of paratroopers in combat. I had served during the "surges" in Iraq and Afghanistan. My last tour in Afghanistan as a commander was particularly trying, as my wife and sons were far from their "home" too; we were based in Alaska, far from our family in the contiguous 48, so while I was gone, they were somewhat isolated and adrift. My fellow commanders and I had lost soldiers and our wives were back home, assisting grieving families while serving as single moms caring for our own. The latter half of my Army career (which had been 20 years and counting, at this point) had been a wild ride for the Campbells. I had been serving in demanding airborne units, which have reputations of high operational tempo at home station, the rigors and stressors of combat notwithstanding. My family and I had endured separation, lost friends and survived through trying times. We desired a more peaceful life, one where we could stop moving every few years. We wanted to buy a house and furniture that would not undergo the beating of frequent moves, and we wanted to watch our youngest son, Louden, complete his high school years in one school and achieve a greater peace.

We were emotional, but we tried to also be practical. I had reached the 20th year of my military career, so a pension was now in the cards. We could close out this chapter of our lives and move on to greener pastures where I wouldn't have to earn a ton of money to be comfortable. The thought of never deploying again, and of gaining better control over parts of my life, was appealing. Years before, I had attempted to stay at Fort Bragg, where we owned a house, and where my wife, Leslie, worked and envisioned a life in North Carolina — a state we had grown fond of, living in the mountains or at the beach or both. My hope was to command a battalion there instead of freezing-cold Alaska, to close out my time in the military and ride off into the sunset.

Squadron Command, 1-40 Cavalry, Airborne (Fort Richardson, AK, 2008).

Besides, I didn't like Colonels. That's right, I said it. Mr. Brigade Commander, Colonel (Retired) Campbell didn't like Colonels. How's that for hypocrisy? I found them somewhat grouchy, overly career-focused, maneuvering, often behind each other's backs, for selection to Brigadier General. In fairness, they were not all like this. In fact, many of them were fine soldiers and people I held in high regard. Fairness aside, though, it was an assessment that contributed to my initial decision to separate as a Lieutenant Colonel (a decision that, you will find as you read further, didn't quite "stick"). Once a Colonel and Brigade Commander, some of those perceptions became reality. It seemed that the difficultly of advancing to the rank of general officer resulted in some Colonels "spotlighting" them-selves. I'm always cautious when I stereotype but I owe you, the reader, what I felt and witnessed. I was not alone in this assessment. Politics and power-hungry maneuvering entered the equation more as we were gaining rank and becoming the military equivalent of executives in a large corporation. And when I thought of where I was headed in my own career trajectory in the military, I wasn't fond of the jobs outside of Brigade Command for Colonels. I witnessed one too many Colonels being flogged by enormous task loads and impatient Generals, and it put a bad taste in my mouth.

Following our tour in Alaska (2008-2010), my family and I were stationed in Germany at a training center where we could catch our breath, take in Europe and reconnect. I went as far as "deciding to retire" but had not put pen to paper or fingers to keyboard to craft a retirement letter to my chain of command. I never crossed the threshold of telling the Army I was done.

Leslie and Rob atop Germany's highest peak, Zugspitze (2011).

To do this, I knew, was permanent. And I had a very clear, reasonable fear. You see, there were plenty of officers like me and putting out the "I'm outta' here" signal would make it easier for the Army at the next promotion and command selection board. When choosing who to promote, they'd have fewer candidates to choose from. Because once I presented this letter, the Army would place my file in the "do nothing with him" batch ... a place I never wanted to be. I wanted my final months or years in the Army to be on my own terms, and leaving when we were in Germany just didn't feel right.

To this day, I'm not sure of the moment when Leslie and I changed our minds. I do recall a meeting with our financial advisor, where he spoke as if we had accepted the fact that the Army was likely to promote me, factoring in my Colonel retired pay into the long-term Campbell plan. We didn't correct him (i.e., didn't mention that I might retire as an LTC with a lower pay), though inside we were both acutely aware of the separation discussions we were having. In fact, I had announced the decision to both of our families and some of my trusted peers, just not my immediate boss and the Army. I believe this was the beginning of our discussions about staying in for a few more years.

Emotions at bay, we were able to think through this logically. The greatest parts of the Army were tugging at us and they were large contributors to our decision to stay. I knew that separating as a Lieutenant Colonel would mean that I would need to go to work immediately in the civilian world, chasing a paycheck and doing so quickly. It was 2011 and our two sons were still in high school, so the college years (tuition, room and board, dorm room swag) were coming. Coupled with this would be a mortgage, a second car, etc. We talked about and listed the great benefits of military life. We knew we needed to do this formally as a way to step back and examine it in order to make a more informed decision. As I remember it, here are the major points of our discussions back then. I think they are all key topics that anyone should consider as they examine the option of departing from a military career.

Housing on a secured base. Leaving the military meant leaving this kind of housing and this kind of community. Military base housing, much of it drastically improved from the days of the 1960s-era patched-up dwellings of my early years, was pretty sweet. I never worried about repairs and main-

The Campbells sell their house in Fayetteville, NC (Fort Bragg), and begin a 2 ½-week road-trip to Alaska.

tenance, which I knew (now more than ever) was a burden I would assume with home ownership once I retired from the Army. Whether it was a water heater on the fritz or a window that wouldn't function or even a lightbulb that needed replacing, there was one number to call or one place to visit.

There were also community benefits that our sons enjoyed. The Army would house us near people of similar rank, which meant our kids were typically neighbors with other kids their same age. Moreover, we would be assured assistance through our moves, if we ever had to leave the home behind for a trip or if, God forbid, something happened to me. These housing developments, for the most part, were on a gated, secured military community. That brought us much comfort. Leaving the Army meant leaving this comfort behind.

30 days a year in paid leave. This meant a lot, as we usually took several weeks off when we moved from one location to another. These were fantastic family moments, where we would travel together and live like kings after the Army threw money at us to fund the

Robbie and Louden in Dingle Harbor, Ireland (Thanksgiving 2010).

move. Such relocation assistance and paid time off would likely be a thing of the past once I transitioned to a civilian career.

Life, medical and dental insurance. Sure, we were paying for that but our portion of the premiums was pennies compared to what it might be on the outside. These insurance payments in the Army had been coming out of my monthly pay and I never had to think of them or worry that a medical procedure might not be covered. The practical expenses of civilian life were something we needed to plan for and worry about.

A chance to travel more and see more places. Though the thought of settling down was exciting, we did enjoy being moved to some great spots like Hawaii, Alaska and Germany. We knew that if I stayed in the Army, there might be another great assignment out there for us, which would add another amazing chapter to an already fulfilling career. The thought of moving (again) had not yet become too distasteful.

Money. While I certainly could make more on the outside, O-6 pay was damn good. It was a nice jump from O-5 pay, not to mention the retirement, which would give us far more options. Pay was not everything, but this difference could not be ignored. Staying a little longer would make a significant financial impact.

Living in a values-based society. While I had no experience living and working in the private sector before joining the Army, I sensed a void at the thought of leaving the military to enter the civilian world. During my decades in the Army, I had grown more alien to my own family, as some of them remained in my hometown ... building their own lives and navigating their own careers, yet serving mainly themselves. I just couldn't relate. They were not part of a "cause" and perhaps didn't see the organization they served (as employees or volunteers) as the priority over their own self-interests and needs. "Working" in the military is fundamentally different from working in most civilian roles, and I knew nothing else. I had a theory that my family and I would suddenly be immersed in a sort of "self-serving" community if we chose to separate, and I wasn't sure I was ready for that. We didn't know what to expect from civilian communities; on the other hand, we could predict with certainty what military communities would be like and the values they upheld.

Was it all that bad? I did enjoy soldiering, especially the infantry and the airborne. Sure, there were moments when it sucked, but what stuck in my memory were the moments when I basked in the magnificence of being part of something larger than myself. At this point in my considerations for separation, I couldn't help but think "I should just stay in" — that very suggestion I made to you at the beginning of this book chapter. You see, I had a theory in my career and I have pondered the theory many times, especially when the going was tough. The theory goes a little something like this: *When the Army sucked, there was nothing worse. It sucked with capital letters, an exclamation point and a bull horn. But when it was great, there was absolutely nothing better.* So, with that theory in mind, I decided — with Leslie's significant involvement in that decision — that our post in Germany would not be our last. I knew I was very much attracted to serving a cause and I knew there were great, inspiring days ahead. I decided I was not ready to say goodbye to the mission and the lifestyle. So we pressed on, with renewed energy and commitment.

THE PERILS OF EMOTIONAL DECISION-MAKING

Emotional decision-making usually leads to bad outcomes. Author, social worker and thought leader Amy Morin argues that excitement, anxiety, sadness, anger and embarrassment are emotions that can screw up decisions.[1] And I think she's right. When we were wrapping up our experience in Alaska in 2010 (much of which I spent on deployment to Afghanistan), we were still healing the wounds of separation and knew too well that more would be on the way in a career dotted with my short and extended departures. While Alaska proved to be an amazing experience for us, my family suffered during my departure. My wife was left to raise our children and care for a squadron of families, which was especially difficult during times when we experienced the death of our soldiers.

---

1   Amy Morin, 13 Things Mentally Strong People Don't Do: Take Back Your Power, Embrace Change, Face Your Fears, and Train Your Brain for Happiness and Success, William Morrow Paperbacks, 2017.

There was, I confess, a bit of anger or resentment toward the Army. It would not sympathize with the hardship it asked of my family and me. The Army would soon be back for more, likely another tour to Afghanistan, agnostic of this hardship. Sadness was prevalent in this period of raw emotions too. So we sought out ways to feel happy and hopeful, and musing about my departure gave us that temporary "high." When we thought of greener pastures, a location and home of our choosing, the freedoms we would enjoy untethered from the grips of the military, we got excited. Mixed in with all that anger, resentment, sadness, excitement and hope was a deep anxiety felt by us all. We were, as we had been time and time again, anxious as we wondered about the future, my promotion, the next high school and a base we would either love or hate. This time, however, we might have a way to squash this anxiety once and for all.

In the Army, we often talk about taking the "hard right instead of the easy wrong." I think that Leslie and I ultimately realized that departing from Army life at that point, while it would have addressed some of our anxieties, would have been the "easy wrong." So, a year into our tour in Germany, just before the Army would decide whether to promote me to Colonel, we opted to stay in. I credit our acknowledgment of these feelings and logic we applied to such a big decision. Once decided, the emotions didn't necessarily disappear, nor was it a shining moment of clarity. It just felt more right than wrong. As it turns out, there was so much more of my Army experience yet to come. In 2012, I would be promoted to Colonel at the end of our tour in Germany and selected for command of an infantry brigade. Looking back on this, I could have tossed it all away and I am thankful that I did not. And, as it turns out, we Colonels aren't so bad!

. . . .

The emotions didn't necessarily disappear, nor was it a shining moment of clarity. It just felt more right then wrong.

. . . .

LOOKING BACK ...

Looking back at this important period of my career, where I almost hung up the uniform, I recall the emotions I was feeling (and the emotions Leslie, Robbie and Louden were feeling too!) and how it seemed to be an inopportune moment to decide on something so important. I was raw from my second deployment, we were catching our breath in Germany (a goldmine of an assignment) and it seemed to me, at first, that conditions were ripe for transition. I thought: *"Enjoy the riches of Germany. Go out on top, having commanded paratroopers in combat, make my own decision and not let the Army tell me it was over."* But those thoughts were fleeting. It wasn't time.

While it was helpful to remember the pain associated with deploying to war, it was a bad time to make a decision with permanent implications. I believe what Leslie and I got right was not rushing to a decision. I never drafted my letter. I delayed, perhaps out of fear or because there was an alternative voice inside me, fighting to be heard which said, *"Not yet."* One of the rules I used was to determine just how long I could delay informing my leadership and the Army of my desire to separate. I was still giving my all, as I had planned to do up to the day I bid farewell. There was no need to rush this. Most senior service-members can recall a time (or many times) in their careers when a leader made an emotional decision, creating negative reper-cussions. I didn't want to be part of that population. I realized my decisions affected others, and I wanted the impact of my decisions to be minimally disruptive for my fellow soldiers, in addition to being positive for me and my family

In retrospect, I can also admit that had I left the Army in 2010 when the idea first crossed my mind (a full six years before my actual separation in 2016), I would have done so before growing into the leader I was capable of being. In truth, I believe I needed to mature a bit as a person and as a leader, and my final years of service allowed me to do that. I recall very vividly that, once I was selected for Colonel and brigade command, I experienced a moment of true inner peace. Indeed, I felt all the anxiety one would feel achieving such a prestigious rank and position, yet I felt that I had arrived. I had overcome all the obstacles the Army could throw at me. I took all the hard assignments and thrust myself into groups of officers I believed to be smarter and more talented than I. I had even survived a few bad bosses. I was going to move forward my way — the way I really wanted to lead and command. (And if the Army would not accept my way, they could ask me to leave but I would do so with a sound retirement and my pride intact.) Looking back, I know that the starts and stops in our "should I stay or should I go" considerations were perfectly normal, and I am thankful we arrived at the right decisions at the right times. I'm glad we stayed as long as we did.

Chapter 2
MAKING THE CALL

Making the final call to retire was anything but easy. I always thought it would be much easier, especially because Leslie and I had been through the intellectual exercise before. I figured I would know when the road had ended and would be able to make the call with ease, using some predetermined criteria such as a degradation of my physical ability required for the rigors of the profession. After all, the infantry was hard on a body. Maybe a post-military job opportunity would present itself and help make the decision easy. As it turns out, none of those things occurred. I was still very physically able enough to lead soldiers — scoring in the high 290s (out of 300) on the Army Physical Fitness Test. I possessed some very relevant experience in operations and warfare, which I could apply at more senior levels, and there was never a knock on my door followed by a lucrative dream-job offer.

So I kept moving forward. The feelings I grappled with during our Germany assignment — those questions about whether it was time to hang up the uniform — had quieted when I was at the U.S. Army War College in 2012-2013, earning another Master's degree, and when I was stationed in Fort Campbell, KY, and deployed to Afghanistan as a brigade commander with the 101st Airborne. But in 2015, those questions were resurfacing as I reunited with my family in Colorado.

My recent tour (2014-15) in Afghanistan had been a particularly challenging one, and I was worn down from what was an arduous decade of training for and fighting wars. You would think this might have been the straw to break the camel's back, helping me craft that letter to my superiors and the Army ... but it still wasn't. In Germany in 2010, following squadron command, I was confident of making Colonel. I didn't believe brigade command was in the cards so I had to wrestle with what I wanted to do if not selected for command. Void of a command opportunity, I convinced myself I would find the best Colonel-level assignment following my probable promotion in 2012 and make a difference. This time, fall of 2015, fresh from my brigade command tour, the decision would be to compete for Brigadier General or transition out. I often heard a former general-officer boss of mine state, when promoting officers to the rank of Colonel, "If your ego is in check, you'll recognize this as your last promotion." For those who make it, Colonel is the final rank. His words spoke to the difficulty of achieving the rank of Brigadier General, one of the toughest promotions to achieve. His words rang very clear in my ears. Indeed, there were no sure bets and I did not believe then (or now) that I was a shoe-in for such a rank. I really didn't. This said, I had to believe in myself and believe that I had a shot (as much of a shot as any of my peers, anyway). To think otherwise was to accept defeat, something I was not programmed to do. All of this in context, still the Army would not be quick to cast me aside. I could serve as a Colonel for several more years in a variety of assignments if I decided to stay.

Following brigade command, I was required to serve in a joint assignment with sister services like the Air Force and Navy. I joined U.S. Northern Command (NORTHCOM), in Colorado, a joint command which would fulfill this requirement. At NORTHCOM, I was assimilating quickly into my new job and was confident I would be adding

more and more value to the team before long. I was at the beginning
of two mostly predictable years, tethered to this command serving
out my joint requirement.

Now in my joint assignment, for the first time in my career I was in
a position to consider the possibilities of becoming a general officer.
As a Brigadier General. I would be a senior executive in the Army
institution, able to cast wide influence and take my leadership and
practices to a new level. To even have a shot at achieving this rank,
I would have to seek a sponsor. Not a sponsor in a formal sense but
a serving General, preferably an Army 4-star to speak my name in
the promotion board, to be my personal champion, "We need Rob
Campbell!" I didn't have anyone in mind but figured I would have to
serve as an executive officer to a 4-star to prove my worth and earn
his or her blessing. A voice inside me kept saying, *"Give it a shot!"*
Why not give it a shot? But my gut was telling me something else, and
so began my internal conflict once again.

MORE STARS, MORE STRIPES?

In the fall of 2015, with our youngest son, Louden, settled into his
last year of high school in Colorado Springs, Leslie and I came to
enjoy more freedom in this job than in previous ones. We began
to discuss the next step very seriously. The conversations were
wonderful, at times, as we spoke with excitement about a great
future. At other times, they became tense and emotional as I wrestled
with my internal conflict or when we disagreed on something.
I felt a gravitational pull to never quit, to keep going, to serve the
Army institution forever and ever. Still reeling from my selection to
command a brigade and the fresh experience of having commanded
one, this next rank, Brigadier General, would represent the unimag-
inable. My doubts remained high but again, I needed to try or not.
Promotion to this rank would have been a wonderful stroke to my

ego — that demon inside me, which returned often, especially when faced with a tough decision. My ego was a hungry fellow, and he wanted a big dose of general officer and was sitting at the table with fork and knife in hand, napkin tucked into his collar, waiting to be fed. I had soldiers standing on my shoulder, whispering in my ear, "Stay and be my champion, I want to serve with you again." Lastly, but not least, I wanted to continue to shape the Army as I believed it needed to be. We had our imperfections and, though I knew I would not be able to fix everything, I would certainly have a bigger voice and influence as a General. All of this was in my DNA. I couldn't shake it. How could I not give this a shot?

Of course, Leslie was having none of it. Nor should she have. What I shared with her, my true authentic voice, should have been (and eventually was) the voice I needed to hear. My career to date had been a somewhat predictable one. Following the infantry officer template developed by Army Human Resource Command, I climbed the mountain of rank-and-command assignments culminating in my field grade years as a Colonel and brigade commander. This new path, if I chose it and was even selected, would take me from the infantry and place me in "generalship." I would possess a broader aperture required for service over large, diverse Army and Joint organizations.

But, when I wasn't romanticizing it, I knew that being a Brigadier General could be life-changing. I had witnessed the life of Generals. Having served as an aide de camp, I was up close and personal with my boss and was able to see first-hand the demands the military placed on him and his family. I admired his ability to handle the enormity of his position and responsibilities. If anything, it taught me that the demands were manageable. However, in a period of perpetual war during my field-grade years, the pace grew unrelenting. I saw no signs of it letting up. I had recently interacted with Generals in Afghanistan and they looked mentally and physically trampled. These men and women were working 18-hour days in the bowels of an unyielding combat zone. I knew that duty like that would be frequent in my future and take years off my life. As a Brigadier general, I would be the "private" of the general officer ranks, at the beck and call of other higher-ranking Generals and of the Army at large, regardless of my personal or family situation.

If I became a general officer, Leslie and I would PCS (i.e., make more permanent changes of station or "move") with far greater frequency (typically every 12 months). I would surely be called to a new assignment almost overnight upon being promoted, leaving Leslie behind alone to pack up our treasured belongings to join me later at our new base (if I was even there and not shipped out already). The Army "machine" would take and take. I couldn't just opt in and then decide to pull the plug a year down the road. My timeline to pin on a star, if selected, would likely be three or more years down the road. Then I would be committed for *another* three years or so to fulfill my commitment of service and acceptance of rank. To increase my chances for Brigadier General, I would have to seek an executive officer (XO) job alongside a 4-star (not an easy job to get), which would be hugely demanding and I could not promise I would find the right 4-Star to serve. There was no assurance we would get along and such a prospect was unattractive; I would be on the losing end of that relationship, in misery, hoping he or she would choose to be my champion in the promotion board.

My selection would surely mean another deployment, this one being a 12-month tour in the bowels of Iraq, Afghanistan or another dangerous, demanding place. I would leave Leslie behind, this time, in empty-nester mode, without our children to support her, alone at a base where she might not feel at home. As was the case with my career to date, there would certainly be more missed anniversaries, family reunions, holidays, birthdays and special occasions. I was approaching 50 and still had lots of fuel in my tank, a lot of life yet to be lived. Like I did with my decision to compete for Colonel and command, I could delay submitting my retirement until the moment I realized promotion would not be in the cards or I would await the Army's directive to retire. I am an optimist and thinking all of this was somewhat alien to me; the idea of being passed over or pushed out was painful to consider. Writing these words in the creation of this book still feels selfish and negative, two things I am not. But these thoughts or analysis, a product of more than 27 years of soldiering, much of it riding shotgun near Generals, could not be ignored. I had to imagine and believe I could make such a rank and consider all the pros of such a selection in order to make an informed decision about our future. But I also had to consider the cons.

I couldn't ignore the impact this career choice — pursuing a future as a general officer — would have on Leslie. As with all our life and career assignments, she embraced most and endured a few. She sacrificed yet was always willing to do that for my betterment, our children's and even our extended Army family. She was always and remains the most selfless person I know. Leslie never had a career in a traditional sense. We did agree that she would stay home and care for our children and we were both content with that decision. Of course, being a stay-at-home mom did equate to a full-time job (with overtime, I would often say). She enjoyed art and really blossomed as an artist in each assignment, especially during our time at Fort Campbell in brigade command. Her studio was always the spare bedroom, the basement or wherever she could find space in the quarters the Army gave us. Unfortunately, she never had the opportunity to plant herself long enough and immerse in a community of artists or gain a following. Just as things began to mature for her, the Army would swoop in and call us to another post. Leslie is an introvert, and I am an extrovert. The social demands of the Army came naturally to me but would sometimes exhaust her. One would never know this, as she navigated our Army social life with grace and self-assurance. However, I knew that the unwritten expectations of her being an active member of each community we served in and the need to be by my side at social events sometimes took its toll. As a general officer's spouse, if we were to go down that path, the social demands on her would multiply and the spotlight over her would shine brighter.

Leslie was transparent with her reservations and I was aware of them. Of course, there was little I could do about this throughout our time in the Army, but now I needed to hear her voice and understand her reservations better than I had before. Leslie never put her foot down or gave me an ultimatum. She would never do that. At the end of the day, we always chose each other and knew we would get through whatever came our way as a united couple. I was deeply grateful for her support yet I still felt a deep sense of duty to make our next journey the best one possible, one where we could watch our family grow and enjoy each other's company with fewer interruptions and where she could finally blossom as an artist. Could I do that as a Brigadier General and beyond? I was feeling pulled toward a civilian life, foreign and scary as it might be.

This all felt very selfish. Leslie and I were institutionalized and proud to be. We were ingrained in an institution, its culture and its values, the Army Values. We had thought no other way for decades but woke up each day in service to the nation, to our servicemembers and their families. It was our life. We were good at this Army stuff and I knew we would make a profound difference in any future assignment. In all that I had done up until this moment, it was never about me. Sure, I had personal desires and worked hard to receive promotions and assignments of my liking, but I would always bow to the needs of the unit and the mission over self. My life's core purpose is to make a difference in the lives of others through optimistic leadership — I knew that about myself when I was in the Army and I know it now. The Army was a perfect fit for a guy like me. But was it perfect forever?

. . . .

My life's core purpose is to make a difference in the lives of others through optimistic leadership — I knew that about myself when I was in the Army and I know it now.

. . . .

As for Leslie, she confessed her selfish hopes and dreams but would always beat them down in gratitude for what she had and what the Army gave to us. We would end some of our discussions without resolution, only able to share and process our thoughts but not arrive at decisions or peace. Was it time to shelve the soundbites of "selfless service, loyalty and mission first?" What was wrong with this philosophy? Why would we jeopardize that to go dabble in the civilian world? Why not throw our hat in the ring for the next promotion? This was hard.

WHAT NEXT?

Of course, talking about whether to stay in and compete for General or retire would be an incomplete exercise if we didn't talk about what we wanted to do next — in *life* and as a couple (not just in the context of work or service to our nation). Indeed "what next" would be a key element in the deciding. We were both educated people. Leslie had a teaching degree and had taught school while we were stationed in North Carolina (Fort Bragg, 2003-2008). I had a business degree and two Master's degrees and a rich resume of commanding large organizations. I had seen other Colonels move into government service jobs, adding that income to their retirement and living comfortably. In fact, I was currently working with several at NORTHCOM, serving as Air Force civilians. Others went into the defense industry, some making very good money. Some senior servicemembers took the contracting route upon their retirement, which often meant leaving family behind for short- to medium-term trips in foreign countries, even Iraq and Afghanistan.

None of that appealed to me. I had served in the military and did not want to come back as a civilian or work as a defense contractor. I held many government civilians in high regard for what they did for the military and leaned heavily on them throughout my career, but it was just not something I wanted to do. I confess the thought of joining a large organization as a corporate-level or "C-Suite" executive did attract me but I couldn't nail down what industry was the right fit. I would get excited thinking about learning a new field and leading a group of people to excellence, using my military leadership methods. I figured I could draw a pretty good compensation package, given my background. Of course, no job discussion would be complete without geography and passion. "Job or geography?" was a question or framework that began to preface many of our discussions. Geography was beginning to dominate.

While stationed in North Carolina (about a decade prior to finding ourselves in Colorado), we fell in love with its coast and mountains. We returned to its coast each summer with family, far beyond our time based there, proof that it was in our blood. We decided that, when we were able to choose our own "home base" — choose our own geography — anywhere in the southeast United States would do the trick, believing that I would likely need to be near a big city for good employment. Coupled with our love for North Carolina was our desire to be closer to our parents, who were in Pennsylvania. Along with our desire to be together often, we envisioned caring for them some day and wanted to be no more than a day's drive to get to them.

As we talked about career aspirations and favorite geography, Leslie and I also kept coming back to a discussion of passion. What was I truly passionate about and could we reside in a place that brought us happiness and also fueled my passion? I had heard many times, and probably stated myself, that after the chaos of a demanding life in the infantry, I would "sweep floors" or "sell shoes" and be content with it. The sound of that brought peace and simplicity but I knew I was not built for that. In fact, I had to listen hard to my core purpose and realize the man who graduated with a business degree back in 1990 was replaced long ago with this seasoned leader, combat veteran and family man. In some ways it was a curse. I couldn't settle for a job that was repetitive, mundane or lacked the opportunity to lead other people. Part of me loved the idea of a job that was peaceful and predictable, but a bigger part of me was terrified by the prospect of it.

. . . .

What was I truly passionate about and could we reside in a place that brought us happiness and also fueled my passion?

. . . .

So, what *am* I passionate about? My interests are in foreign policy, defense issues, writing, leadership and academia. I'm a problem-solver and an entrepreneur (though, when I was in the Army, that's not a word I would have used to describe myself), always looking at things critically and wondering how I could make them better. I love the outdoors, the mountains and the beach, motorcycle riding, music, traveling, fine wine and cold beer. Through this reflection, I felt a burning desire to want to pursue the things I loved with greater desire and frequency. I actually felt a bit of resentment toward the Army for preventing me from embracing and pursuing the things that brought me fulfillment ... I knew this was unfair. Finding fulfillment was up to me. And the Army did provide space for me to pursue much of this, just not when I wanted or for as long as I wanted to. The Army introduced me to and helped me grow some of these passions and I needed to remain grateful. Going forward, these passions had to remain top of mind as I navigated my new journey. But there were already so many other things that were "top of mind" — career interests, geography, lifestyle, passions!

During 2015, while I was settling into my operations officer role at NORTHCOM (Peterson Air Force Base, CO), Leslie and I dedicated a lot of time — most of our waking hours spent together — talking about this decision, debating and hearing each other's points. We had to let our true feelings be known, not only to each other but to ourselves. I had to dig down hard and drag out the things I truly felt. I had to overcome my institutionalism, emotions and ego, and I had to mute the voices of others who were not me and didn't have my true interests at heart. I had to add an extra dose of authenticity to my DNA strands and hear my inner voice. I spent lots of time imagining different futures or envisioning different courses of action (COAs). As I was trained to do so well in the Army, I always strove to develop multiple COAs from which the boss could choose, so as not to box him in. As I did these exercises, different paths started to emerge. I began to see a path forward where I wore a suit and invested in people the way I had done in the Army. I could envision my style of leadership really making a difference with employees in civilian organizations. I could envision a house in the mountains or at the beach, where Leslie could bloom as an artist in her own space — finally free of the threat of moving once again. I could envision a bigger paycheck, which would allow us to pursue some of our life goals of traveling and creating special spaces in our new home — a home of our own choosing in a neighborhood and not on a military installation.

I began to see time with family, uninterrupted birthdays and Christmases, free of my government phone and the grips of military service. This felt real and right. The path that emerged, the one that felt the truest, was different from the path the Army wanted me to take. For the first time in my career, my path and the Army's path began to diverge. I needed to accept it. I needed to convince myself that it was OK. It took time to do that but I did it through frequent reflections and thinking about all Leslie and I had talked about and all I had analyzed. I had a great career and was enormously grateful for all the Army had given me. I had worked hard and had given the Army and its people my very best. I didn't owe them anything more. I had been soldiering faithfully since my enlistment in 1987, most of that on active duty. Army math would have me at 27 years, 5 months and 7 days by the time I officially retired in 2016. That was a long time but it was not a lifetime. I had a long road still to travel — beyond the Army — and I would be better prepared for that road's potholes and detours with all I had experienced. I would take with me all the great things my bosses and the Army had given me and use them in ways that did not require a camouflage uniform. It was time to bid a fond farewell and hit the road for another exciting journey ... armed with the Army Values, strong leadership, a great resume, and my drive and passion to do more and be of service. It was time to retire.

· ·

I would take with me all the great things my bosses and the Army had given me and use them in ways that did not require a camouflage uniform.

· ·

LOOKING BACK ...

Upon reflection, I am glad that Leslie and I were able to talk things out in a way that felt deliberate, rational, thoughtful and somewhat "unemotional" as we approached our final decision. I'm glad we were in the right environment for these discussions. We weren't on opposite sides of the world, with me in a battlefield and calling on a satellite phone, nor were we in the middle of an assignment that left me physically exhausted and too tired to think straight each night. Leslie and I were able to be a true team in making our decision. And this final post at U.S. Northern Command was a perfect one to be my last.

NORTHCOM would not and did not even recognize I was having these thoughts, nor would it care that I desired to move on. In my current role, I could be replaced easily. Looking back, I surely could not have done this as a brigade commander. The demands of that job would not have allowed me to dedicate the time to think through my military departure and come to consensus with Leslie. While I felt that I was a transparent leader, it just would not have felt right to announce my retirement to a brigade of soldiers who I spent so much time trying to convince to stay. Certainly, most would have understood that I was not a Sergeant or Lieutenant making the call after a short career but I would have felt hypocritical being a commander and a good steward of the Army's personnel needs, then taking a knee, as they say. Moreover, I knew we would need about a year to transition if we decided to do so, and sitting on Fort Campbell with the 101st Airborne, going to briefings and out-processing with soldiers I used to command would not work. In NORTHCOM, on the other hand, I could take the time I needed to do this right. That big headquarters would not miss a beat, and they might not even miss *me* once I was gone. I felt a sort of peace with that reality.

Surfacing our real feelings (instead of just my programmed commitment to the Army values and a soldier's ideology) and, yes, even selfish hopes and dreams was a requirement if we were to get this right. Emotions were hard to beat down and, if I could go back and do it all again, I would have invested more time using the tools of my trade — like a decision matrix, listing out pros and cons, knowns and unknowns to make a more informed, unemotional decision. But even with the full academic analysis, I made the right decision. Looking back, I needed the perspective of others who knew me personally and only as an Army Colonel. I thought I might get some push-back but found it was not the case. I had to listen closely to the "hard right" voice — the one of fact, logic and true feelings. The "easy wrong" voice told me to just stay the course. The "hard right" voice told me to move on my desired path and retire. A mentor of mine put it so perfectly. After informing him of my decision, he was very supportive. He knew I was a seasoned leader who had been making decisions in a profession where getting the decision right could mean life or death. He was as confident as I was that I was making the right decision at the right time. Furthermore, he prepared me for the "you're quitting" comment. I was expecting it might come once I made my decision known and after I had an approved retirement from the Army. I never told a retiree they were quitting, but confess the word entered my head. "Quit" was not in my vocabulary or DNA. I had stepped forward where others would not in countless situations, not the least of which was commanding soldiers in combat. I didn't have to do that. There were plenty of opportunities for me to quit throughout my life and career, and I took none of them. This was no different. In fact, I believed it took guts to make the military/civilian transition after two and half decades in service to the Army, and I would take offense to an ignorant comment about "quitting" or pulling up short. Thankfully, it never came. While there were many who were surprised at my decision, they could quickly tell I had thought it out and was not making it in haste. I was supported by friends, family and colleagues alike, and am so grateful for that.

I would take with me all the great things my
bosses and the Army had given me and use them
in ways that did not require a camouflage uniform.

Chapter 3
NOW WHAT?

Hell if I knew! Deciding to retire from the Army, despite all the intellectual and emotional work of arriving at the decision itself, left me feeling a profound sense of "Now what?" As a matter of fact, it felt just like my airborne experience in the 82nd Airborne Division. We would dump countless hours and days preparing for a unit parachute assault. It's a comprehensive and exhausting build-up for an event that would be over in a matter of minutes. I remember vividly, wiping the sweat from my brow after having turned in my chute and saying, "OK, now what was that training event we had planned to follow our jump?" It was one of those moments I had nightmares about. I'm standing in front of a group of paratroopers and they are screaming "What next, sir?" and I have no answer.

The lead-up to my retirement was not quite nightmare material but a foreign space for sure. The abyss, to be more specific. Leslie and I did have the "what next" discussion but it was more generic and focused on mitigating the risk of getting it wrong. We knew our decision was right, but hadn't really thought much about how to announce it and what milestones would need to be achieved before I could grow a beard, play solitaire and send emojis to people.

. . . .

We knew our decision was right, but hadn't really thought much about how to announce it and what milestones would need to be achieved before I could grow a beard, play solitaire and send emojis to people.

. . . .

First things first, I had to inform my boss and the Army that I was moving on. I was still fresh in my assignment at NORTHCOM, having arrived late the previous October. The holidays had just passed and the time off had been a great opportunity to share our thoughts with and seek counsel from family and friends. Now, we found ourselves in the early days of 2016, the year I wanted to be my last in the Army. It was time to formalize this. I got on my boss's calendar to inform him and seek approval for my retirement. It was an office call I had never given much thought to or ever planned for. I thought deliberately about how I would present this news to him. He was a 2-Star General and I didn't know him well beyond my initial days under his leadership.

I decided on a tone of selflessness — an approach which considered the institution over me. I was confident that this universal military language and approach of selflessness would surely be appreciated. I was going to speak to someone who had given and would continue to give of himself for the institution. Making this all about me would not be my approach and, of course, was not who I was anyway. My true self placed the Army institution first, knowing that I would not serve it well unless I was "all in." As I anticipated the meeting with my boss, I was still not sure how he would take the news. Would he see me as a guy who slipped under the radar ... who had scored a cushy assignment to Colorado Springs with the plan to skate during my time there? While transition was on my mind as I shipped the family off to Colorado for my current assignment, I had not yet decided at that point to put in for my retirement. In fact, I needed

this assignment to remain competitive for Brigadier General. When
I took the assignment, I didn't know it would be my last, but here
I was. I wanted to make it clear to my new boss that I did not have the
initial intention of retiring when I accepted the position I was nomi-
nated for. I needed for him to understand that I had every intention
of fulfilling my duty but wanted his approval to retire at the end of the
year, proving my loyalty to contributing to the NORTHCOM cause
and helping him solve some organizational problems. I was essen-
tially giving nearly a year's notice. This would give him time to find
another nominative Colonel or Navy Captain to replace me. I also
wanted him to know that I intended on soldiering all the way up
until the day my orders stated I was a retiree. I had seen others, who
were on their way out, completely lose their sense of duty and military bearing. I had zero intentions of doing that. Lastly, I was ready
to entertain his quest to keep me in the Army if it came to that, and
I was prepared to outline my logic.

I entered the meeting a bit defensive, which I didn't like, but
I didn't know how else to feel in this once-in-a-career moment.
I had my boxing gloves close to me, so to speak, ready to counter
punch a "quit" comment or anything like it, but I was not seeking
a confrontation. I was well prepared to talk about this as a personal
decision — one that was right for my family and for me — regardless
if he could appreciate that or not. I certainly didn't want to come off
as "I'm worn down from years of combat and need to take a knee."
Though I was a bit trodden from years in muddy-boots (or shall I say
dusty-boots) assignments, so too were others, some of whom had far
more deployments than I. I always despised that sentiment, when
leaders on their way out seemed to say, "You and the others can navigate these troubled waters; I'm abandoning ship as my wellbeing is
more important than yours."

As it turns out, the meeting with my boss went fine. He listened
closely and offered his help in the transition, which he understood

would be a big one. I was appreciative and humbled by his understanding and support. Walking out of his office, I was filled with
a strange collection of feelings: relief that I had his backing and
didn't have to defend myself, sadness that I had just sealed my fate
and this proud chapter of my life would soon end, excitement about
the future, and nervousness given the unknown path which lie
ahead. I called Leslie to share the outcome of the meeting and that
night we toasted to a great career, life and future.

While my boss didn't challenge me during my retirement announcement meeting, I know that I owed him and myself transparency
about the decision. If asked or challenged, I would have shared
how grateful I was to be a servicemember and the privileges of
commanding units I would never have dreamt possible. I was grateful
for a life of service to my country and my soldiers and would always
hold the Army in very high esteem. This was to be a fond farewell
and not a bitter divorce. I would have shared my reservations about
the Brigadier General promotion process and the path to get there.
He would have struggled to paint the promotion process as anything
but easy and non-political, and I would have needed him to understand that I could not give my all to that process. If pressed, I would
have explained my family situation with my youngest son graduating
from high school and my wife and I approaching a new phase in our
lives. I would have shared our interest for being near family in the
approaching second half of our lives (both of us approaching 50).
I would have told him of my interest in bringing Army-style leadership into the private sector — using all that leaders like him had
taught me, to make a difference in people around me. I would have
told him that I would continue to serve as an Army ambassador and
help, as so many senior leaders desired to do, decrease the growing
divide between the military and the citizens it serves. The future was
bright and the Army's investment in me, including his and my experience in NORTHCOM, would not be in vain.

PAPERWORK, TO-DO LISTS AND BIG ANNOUNCEMENTS

Next up, after my initial meeting with my boss, I contacted the
NORTHCOM Human Resources Department who coached me
through the retirement process, which included sending a letter to
Army Senior Leader Division (SLD), the department that managed
Colonels. I promptly did this and submitted it to SLD. This letter
would complete my initial steps to start the wheels of change. The
personnel managers would take it from here and follow up with me.
I had PCS'd from dozens of installations, turned in equipment and
moved my family, so closing up shop and saying goodbye was not
new to me. But this one would be far different. I would not only be
turning in military gear and boxing up my belongings, but I would
be leaving the military forever ... moving to a location and a job yet
unknown. *What's the big deal, right? Welcome to the abyss, Campbell!
Put your toes on the edge of the white line and wait to be called.*

Once my retirement was approved and I had some sense of my
separation timeline, I felt obligated to inform many of the people
I had served with and who made a difference in my life. Seeing
no other modern and expedient way to tell so many people, all at
once, that I was retiring, I decided a bulk email would have to do
the trick. I spent some time gathering the addresses for those who
I had commanded and for those who mentored me. It was a tough
email, I confess. The hardest part of the transition would be telling
those who were counting on me that I was ending my service in the
Army. I felt that I would be letting down all those leaders who went
out on a limb for me, who underwrote my mistakes or who gave me
a chance. I wanted to honor their loyalty to me in some way. I was
bound and determined to do that in my next journey.

In writing the email, I knew I could create a dissertation and lay out
the specifics of my decision (but, as you now know, that tale can fill
a book!) or I could keep it short, sweet and appropriate. Below is

precisely what I sent. I wrote several drafts in a Word document then copied and pasted it into the body of an email. My intent behind this note was to ward off the rumor mill from starting and be the first to share the news of my retirement. Justifying myself or offering an apology would have been inappropriate. Indeed, I needed to give the recipients more credit. They were all special to me and my family, and I trusted they would know better than to think I was making this decision in haste.

> *"Family, friends, fellow warriors,*
>
> *I ride off into the sunset the end of this summer after a very fulfilling career and life as a soldier. It's been an incredible journey serving in some of the best units on the best installations in the world. What matters most are the people. We will forever cherish our memories with you, and your love and friendship. Would love to stay in touch, hear about your adventures and help you in any way. My contact info is below. Planning a formal retirement cere-mony early October. Will follow up with an invitation as we get this put together.*
>
> *Wishing you and yours all the very best,*
> *Colonel Rob Campbell"*

I had trust in the process that the Army would take me through and would find out soon enough the next steps. I had heard from others who had been through the retirement process before me that they wish they had started earlier. It was January and this did put me on somewhat of a short timeline if I desired to be in a new place, swinging in my hammock, by fall. I did my research and talked to the transition experts about how to schedule my departure. The bigger questions remained and they began to pile up:

- What about pay, extra leave I had accumulated and terminal leave?

- What about insurance, survivor benefits, VA disability decisions and health and dental insurance once on the outside?
- Would I have to move back to the home of record (Massachusetts) I annotated on a form 27 years ago?

All those answers — and many, many more — would come eventually but I needed to list them out in a "to do" format so I could check them off along the way. Most critical in the early days was scheduling medical appointments so that my records would be updated and everything would be complete by the time I signed off for good.

I did what I always did when facing the unfamiliar — I educated myself. I did this a few ways.

- I signed up for all the transition seminars and briefings the Army and veteran-support organizations offered. I attended Boots to Business and a variety of other briefings, like Survivor Benefit Plan. I participated in the Afterburner Veteran's Transition Seminar hosted by USAA and found it very focused and relevant.
- I met often with my financial advisor to talk about home buying and surviving off my retired income.
- I scheduled the medical appointments I knew I needed so I could repair some of my busted-up parts and get them documented for my transition.
- I read books.
  - *What Color is Your Parachute?* by Richard N. Bolles has a handful of great exercises you can complete to help you determine what it is you really want to do. It is updated frequently.
  - *Down Range* by James D. Murphy and William M. Duke is another good book, which focuses on developing a post-military career.
  - *The 4-Hour Work Week* by Timothy Ferriss was definitely an outlier because he challenges almost every traditional

thought about work and the work week. It's a wonderful read and inspiring. I found Tim's radical approach enlightening and have frequently returned to it to refocus my lifestyle and think more about my future. I was attracted to Tim's courage and audacity and I found that I challenged myself to do the things that Tim had.

- I also read *Rich Dad, Poor Dad* by Robert T. Kiyosaki. This book really helped me think smarter about money. I wrestled with my new income and the challenges life continues to present and found this book helpful overcoming some of those woes.

- Because of my desire to write, an untapped reservoir of creativity lying dormant inside me, my wife recommended *Big Magic* by Elizabeth Gilbert. That's right, the *Eat, Pray, Love* lady. Me, the big burly airborne ranger eating, praying and loving! Well I didn't read *that* book (I probably should) but *Big Magic* unlocked my creative side, a side which I believe exists in many of us. Consider our 43rd President, George W. Bush, who discovered his passion for painting following his departure from the presidency in 2009. I never tapped into my desire to write until I had the time like I had in retirement. It is wonderful and Gilbert's philosophy on creativity was just what this old soldier needed.

- Sebastian Junger's book *Tribe: On Homecoming and Belonging* was published in 2016, the year of my retirement and could not have entered my life at a better time. I came across it in the spring of 2017, deeply immersed in American society, still fresh from my years of service and a deployment that had ended only two years before. It was amazing and I believe *Tribe* ought to be required reading for anyone stepping out of uniform and into civilian society. The book is bursting with theories and comparisons to tribal life and examples of what servicemembers experience in a deeply divided, affluent society like ours — especially when they return from war.

Reading — beyond any other activity I engaged in during and after my transition — really helped me see my next journey through a new lens. I was on the cusp of total freedom. Freedom I had not enjoyed as a servicemember who was always accountable to the military. I read for a variety of reasons and I would recommend the same for you.

. . . .

Reading — beyond any other activity I engaged in during and after my transition — really helped me see my next journey through a new lens.

. . . .

OH, THE PLACES WE COULD GO!

Leslie and I segued from talking about the *decision* to talking about job and geography. Knowing the southeast was in our veins, I began to search job sites and see what big corporations were in or near the big cities. This was a shot in the dark. I really didn't know where to start. Glassdoor.com was a helpful site to be able to view income and see reviews of each organization from current and previous employees, but I suspected the only people who wrote those reviews were the people who *really* loved it or *really* hated it. And I was seeking the truth.

It was all still very early but my curiosity was at its peak. I Googled "executive job search," as I knew I would need to serve at the executive level in an organization, and found a few sites. One described serving as an executive with an income potential exceeding $200,000. I had zero experience in corporate America but knew that I possessed the skills and experience for leadership in a large organization. The prospect sounded sexy and exciting and I needed help getting there. After a few conversations, I signed on with an executive job search agency and proceeded to follow their program, watching videos, conducting exercises and speaking frequently with a networking coach. I set up a new personal email account (my first .com!), which I would use as my primary email following my transition out of the .mil world. I opened a Facebook account. That's right, I went there. My own Facebook account! Or page. Or it is a profile? Yes, that's it. Facebook profile! Talk about milestones. Showing my age. I had been so busy and not interested in social networking, on top of my already loaded schedule, that I never ventured into Facebook until I was looking at 50 and military retirement; admittedly, I was a little late to the game.

Until this moment, I had dismissed the value of social media and online networking. I believe the philosophy was, "I don't need any more friends," or "I don't have time to read about — nor do I care about — everyone's GREAT DAY or OH WOE IS ME posts typed in all capitals with little emoji smiling cats and flying birds. I'm too important and busy defending the nation." That was me. Not all my peers were like that. In fact, as I was departing the military, many of my friends were on Facebook and it was a great way for me to keep in touch. And I knew, early on, that if I were to make a name for myself or want to connect to new people and communities in that massive world outside the gates of my current military installation, I would have to start social networking.

I decided I would sign up for all that the Transition Assistance Program (TAP) offered, whether I believed I needed it or not. I didn't want to take on an attitude of "I don't need that shit ... I'm a Colonel!" Transition was an area I paid little attention to aside from helping other soldiers transition during my career. I needed it; I needed a chance to explore all my options. For instance, I had not decided at that point that I would start my own business but

I participated in Boots to Business anyway. It was a bit elementary but it was free and might help me generate some ideas. I knew the services had placed a lot of emphasis on transition, especially the Army because it paid unemployment insurance, a huge bill and a cost that I imagined the Army wanted to significantly decrease. However, I discovered that most all of the transition programs were geared toward younger servicemembers who would most definitely seek employment immediately after their separation. I was in a different category. While information about starting your own business and job seeking assistance instruction was decent, I was not feeling the pressure of having to sprint toward a job. Part of the thrill of retirement, for me, was the time and freedoms I would gain.

. . . .

Part of the thrill of retirement, for me, was the time and freedoms I would gain.

. . . .

Given the operational tempo I had been under for so many years, the thought of rushing to a 60-hour work week was not very exciting. This void I felt in the transition process is part of the reason for this book. There wasn't a good document, seminar or book geared for senior servicemembers retiring with a pension. I was able to speak to a retired general officer during the Afterburner seminar but, in most of the events I attended, I felt like the minority amongst younger servicemembers departing with fewer than 10 years of service. I appreciated the focus on them but most of the content being offered simply wouldn't help me. To fill this gap, I reached out to a few mentors who had made the transition as senior servicemembers and were well into the next phases of their lives. The conversations were enormously helpful and I took copious notes.

Here is some great advice I received from my friend Tim Scully, a mentor and a retired Colonel with whom I had served when he was a Colonel on a General's staff and I a budding young Major. "Congratulations on your tremendous first career," were the opening words in his email to me. "Don't look back. Don't run *away* from anything — run *toward* something." The "first career" and "run toward something" comments really made me think. It was true Tim wisdom. He always delivered the most profound and useful input in the room, which I feverishly copied into my Army green book. This time was no different. Once again, he was right. I was not finished. I never felt I was done running the race but I confess I spent a lot of time looking back, reflecting on what I had done, what I got right and what I got wrong. I needed to look through the windshield and not the rearview mirror, and Tim knew (somehow) that I needed to hear that. "You are at the top of your game. Great time to shift from a known point and reinvent yourself. Don't second-guess yourself. You know when it is the right time and place to make the transition. Go forward and attack the next challenge." Wow, nicely put and spot on. Of course, as always, I plagiarize that when it comes my time to coach others on the transition as he has coached me.

I connected with Tim on a long phone call and here are some of the points he shared. I still have the notes.

- Figure out what you want to do, where you want to live and how much you want to make.

- Be careful touting your service and the level of responsibility you had. Most civilians have not led to the scale you have, and you might overwhelm a potential employer who may have only led what you consider to be a squad or a small platoon.

- You might be underwhelmed by what an employer asks you to do. "That's it?" might be your thought.

LOOKING BACK ...

As I look back on the steps I took in making my retirement intentions known and official, I'm glad I took the approach I did with my boss — the honesty, the clarity about my unflagging commitment to serving and soldiering up until my very last day. Perhaps my maturity and years as an officer paid off. I'm sure I stole someone's approach and labeled it my own but this is the beauty of learning from others. (I still use sayings and concepts someone else developed.) I'm also glad I got advice from others all along the way. While confident in my decision and knowing it would be me and me alone to sign the paperwork, it was helpful to seek the counsel of others. No need to go it alone.

If I could go back and do it all over again, knowing what I know now, I would have entered the social media space much earlier. I should have transitioned with a very mature social network — on LinkedIn, Facebook and elsewhere — but instead found myself building it as my facial hair grew. I also wish I had done some reading earlier. The thought of retirement was certainly on my mind, but I did little about it. An earlier education would have helped. Hence the reason for this book!

And if I can offer a direct piece of advice: Save your military contact list! In an instant, I was off the .mil email network where I had years of contacts. I found myself suddenly in Gmail, a foreign space for sure. I saved some emails but was never very diligent in collecting addresses throughout my years. I wished I had invested more time in this. You just never know who you might want to reconnect with via email, for advice or to say thank you. And from a practical standpoint, when it came time to send my "mother-of-all emails," announcing my retirement, it was hard to gather up contact information for all those I wanted to inform.

Chapter 4
KEEPING IT REAL

Welcome to the heart of this book or, in military parlance, the Main Effort. Thus far I've shared some sage thoughts on the military/civilian transition for senior servicemembers and the practicalities of such a major change in your life. In an attempt to "keep it real" with you, I'd like to spend some time addressing authenticity and creativity, suggesting you cast aside old assumptions, urging you to challenge traditional paths, reminding you that it's okay to open yourself up and wrestle with that big ego monster (which lives in all of us). This chapter will help you turn from the crowd and choose your own path, one that fits *you* and not one that everyone else (especially those still serving in the military) thinks you ought to travel. There will be plenty of "help" in your days approaching retirement and long after. Listen to all of it but be cautious of drifting off course. Along with a nice paycheck and new house, you might also find unhappiness. Reflecting on my transition and hearing the stories of dozens of transitioned servicemembers, it dawned on me that the armed services and those who run the transition programs are asking the wrong question: "What do you want to do?" Instead, they should be asking: "Who are you?"

. . . .

The armed services and those who run the transition programs are asking the wrong question: "What do you want to do?" Instead, they should be asking: "Who are you?"

. . . .

If you're like me, you have served decades (maybe even three or four of them) in a very traditional organization. While innovation and change have been prevalent across our military, especially in the conduct of modern warfare, much remains unchanged in the big bureaucracies we serve or served in. Military traditions, while rich in history and deserving of preservation, cause us to become traditional and standard in our approaches to everything. This can squash creative career and life thinking. In the military, while we might not know what base we will live on next or what our next assignment might be, we generally know what to expect in terms of our career paths. Show up, work hard, get promoted and advance on a somewhat-rigid progression. Navigating this does not require much creativity. Career paths in the military are created for us in a system that scientifically manages people based on the needs of the branch of service and the occupational skill(s) of the servicemember. Your passion is decided for you. You might be passionate about pottery or furniture building but your military career expects you to perform your prescribed duties regardless of these passions. Many of us are lucky that we found passion alignment with our military careers and achieved fulfillment. I was one of those lucky ones, but the rigid, predictable path and job expectations I became accustomed to were soon to vanish.

In the military, while we might not know what base we will live on next or what our next assignment might be, we generally know what to expect in terms of our career paths. Show up, work hard, get promoted and advance on a somewhat rigid progression. Navigating this does not require much creativity.

In the summer of 2013 (three years prior to my eventual retirement), I was fortunate to have considerable time to reflect and prepare for command of a brigade in the 101st Airborne Division. I was to take the reins of an infantry brigade just shy of 5,000 soldiers in a highly deployable division during a time of war. Coupled with this,

Rob accepting the colors and command of the 327th Infantry Regiment, 1st Brigade, 101st Airborne Division, Air Assault (2013).

the Army, writ large, was suffering from a host of social and behavioral issues. Sexual assault and harassment were on the rise and the Army was in the early stages of addressing it. Suicides had surpassed combat deaths and soldiers were lacking resilience and coping skills to deal with relationship issues, the pressures of life and wartime service and PTSD. It was an environment ripe for a strong, compassionate, transparent and self-aware leader. This caused me to do some deep introspection.

One night that summer, while having drinks with some Army colleagues, I was struck by the approach one of the leaders took with his organization. He developed what he called a biography sketch (or BIO sketch) to share with his soldiers and asked that they create ones to share with him. This sketch, quite different from the standard biography we have all seen (which details jobs, titles, assignments, qualifications and awards), would serve as an open book. I instantly fell in love with the idea and believed it to be perfect for the organization I was soon to command. So I wrote one. My BIO sketch described who I was as a person, influences from my childhood, life crucibles I had experienced, what I believed to be my weaknesses and strengths, how I received and processed information, and what my personality traits and indicators meant. The sketch included my life's core purpose and some of my passions, like adventure motorcycling and time at the beach. With all its positives and negatives, it was (and still is) the true me and while it helped me prepare for command, it also served as a personal vision or guiding light for me to use in my post-military life too.[1]

As part of my preparation that summer, I was also fortunate to attend a seminar called True Growth (TruthGrowthLeadership.com), which took me through a weekend of introspection and quest for authenticity. I found this to be of enormous value. I would later bring the seminar to my brigade and my leaders raved about it. The big outcome of this seminar for me? Clarity about my life's core purpose. Stated again: *To make a difference in the lives of others through optimistic leadership.* This was truly why I was placed on this earth and it would be something I needed to pursue far beyond my military service. I still have a little card in my wallet that articulates this purpose and I mention it often when speaking about authenticity and my post-military journey. Knowing who you are and the purpose you fulfill makes it so much easier to know where to go and what to do next.

---

1   You can see my full biography sketch at RobCampbellLeadership.com/Book.

. . . .

Knowing who you are and the purpose you fulfill makes it so much easier to know where to go and what to do next.

. . . .

CONSTANTLY SEEKING PASSION-FOCUS AND CLARITY OF "MISSION"

As a commander, I had made it my policy to speak with every officer who wanted to separate from the service before I would approve their separation. I did this to help the Army keep its best on the team but also to ensure my leaders were seeking something true and authentic. It was my duty to retain our best officers but I wanted to ensure they were pursuing happiness and not something fake or misaligned with who they really were, what they were passionate about and what would bring them fulfillment. Some learned that the military was the right place for them. Others had external pressures and family obligations causing them to consider a different path. I would always ask what it was they liked and disliked about the Army. I would attempt to draw out their true passion and steer them toward that ... even if it meant separation from service. I found that too many officers had not considered their true passion. They let location, a paycheck or some other notion of a greener pasture guide them and they sometimes missed what it was they truly loved doing. For some it was, in fact, soldiering. My loyalty was to that purpose and passion, not the Army. If one was not fulfilled in the Army, then I saw it as my duty to help him or her transition to something more authentic.

Now it's your turn. You're reading this book, so welcome to my proverbial office. I understand you want to transition from the military. Thank you and your family for a life spent in a noble and honorable profession. I approve your transition but let's make sure you get this life-changing move right. We'll start by discovering why you were placed on this earth and what you are truly passionate about. To focus on anything else at this stage would put your true happiness at risk.

Do you know what your core purpose is? What you're passionate about? Who you are? You need to find out, be sure and then let that clarity guide you.

. . . .

Do you know what your core purpose is? What you're passionate about? Who you are? You need to find out, be sure and then let that clarity guide you.

. . . .

My core purpose remains central to what I do and want to do. I remember, vividly, pulling the card from that authenticity seminar out and reviewing my notes shortly after my retirement was approved. In January of 2017, I attended a weekend gathering of entrepreneurs who spent the days skiing and the afternoons "master-minding" about their lives and businesses. I was impressed and inspired by the tenacity of these people and their sense of purpose. There, I met Jim Hughes. Jim is the Untamed Entrepreneur. I was still very fresh in my post-military journey, having officially retired the previous fall so the timing for me to meet Jim was great. Jim and I were in a small group of entrepreneurs, talking about our lives and journeys. We shared our passions and personal and professional challenges. Jim and I had a side conversation and struck up an immediate friendship. Jim is British, in his 30s and never served in the military but I found him refreshing and laser focused in the pursuit of an authentic life. He became my life coach and remains a superb sounding board as I attempt to maximize my talent and live a purposeful life. Where I used to have a military mentor on my shoulder, whispering in my ear and steering me in leadership, I now have Jim steering me in my passions and business ventures.

On the surface, it looks like a horrible match. What qualifies
a young, non-military British lad to coach a seasoned U.S. Army
officer, combat veteran, husband and father of two grown men? And
that's just the point. I need no coaching on leadership, raising children or advice on marriage. But I do need coaching and perspective
when it comes to the pursuit of and loyalty toward my passions and
business ventures in this new civilian space I occupy. Jim has quite
a story of his own. He has done things I have not and experienced
life crucibles in his own journey, which brought him to his current
role. I find him of tremendous value and I am not alone. Jim coaches
several people, including a retired United Kingdom Army 2-Star
General seeking many of the same things I am. Jim's got game.

Jim has taught me that what is most important for us all, but especially for those of us crafting encore lives and careers, is *reaching our
potential and living in a state of fulfillment.* Read that again — now is
the time in your life for you to reach your potential and live in a state
of fulfillment. It's time to enjoy the freedoms you fought for.

Jim has a tried-and-true methodology for helping his clients to gain
clarity and move in the right direction. He taught me to focus on four
foundational steps:

- **STEP 1:** "NOW" — Where are you now?
- **STEP 2:** "YOU" — Know yourself.
- **STEP 3:** "WHY" — Uncover your mission.
- **STEP 4:** "WHO" — Define your customer.

I think Jim's insights are vital for transitioning servicemembers so
I asked him to do us all the honor of writing a few pages about how
we can get "from here to there" during our military/civilian transitions. And, generous as he is, he happily obliged. Check out this
book's Special Contribution, written by Jim Hughes and entitled
"Reaching Our Potential and Living in a State of Fulfillment." In the

military, I was given my mission. In my new life, the mission was mine to create. Finding a mentor like Jim has been crucial to aligning my efforts to a new mission ... to *my* mission. It is my hope that this book gives you some food for thought, some tools, some suggestions and some nudges in the right direction to find *your* new mission too.

LOOKING BACK ...

Turn from the crowd. Yup, I did that. But man, this stuff is hard work! Reflecting on this part of the transition, I was thankful to have discovered my core purpose and to have engaged in some introspection and self-awareness. My brigade command preparation and experience taught me to be more self-aware. Without that experience, being directed to attend the True Growth seminar, I believe I would have entered my encore life ill informed. It is why I spend a majority of my time coaching transitioning veterans to discover their own "why." Retiring with my core purpose in hand was still not enough though. Looking back, I'm even more convinced that my transparency and willingness to let Jim Hughes into my life (and then choosing him as my life coach) was one of my wiser decisions. He helps me take my core purpose far beyond a just statement I can regurgitate. He helps me put into action. Again, it's not all a bed of roses, this journey, but what my reflections have taught me is that by letting my guard down, by opening up to someone I believed could help — someone far different from me — I'm happier and healthier. I needed a battle buddy in the Army. I need another one, save for the battle, in this next chapter of my life.

> It's not all a bed of roses, this journey, but what my reflections have taught me is that by letting my guard down, by opening up to someone I believed could help — someone far different from me — I'm happier and healthier. I needed a battle buddy in the Army. I need another one, save for the battle, in this next chapter of my life.

This stuff is hard work. Did I mention that? I'm approaching the 4th anniversary of my retirement, but I still need to return to my core purpose, often. I still need to "see" myself. I've completed a variety of self-awareness exercises and honed this skill as an executive leadership coach and it has helped me tremendously. I can't imagine transition without it. I still need Jim and the other new mentors I have in my life to put me in check, counter my old senior officer traditional ways and teach me. I still need greater self-awareness, better than I did in uniform, wrestling with my Colonel identity in a non-military world, identifying my flow-state, when my energy is up and I'm confident and fulfilled. I have to listen to and feel this physical and mental state as a reminder of what is authentic and important. I have to do this with each job offer, opportunity or detour (which might just wind up becoming a traditional, unimaginative and unfulfilling path).

What I'm describing is vulnerability as a person and a leader. After decades leading, I only came to realize it through my post-military studies and readings on leadership. I've listened to Jim and sometimes blew him off. Leslie and I still examine the journey we are traveling, including the possibility of pursuing more traditional, predictive paths. I don't want to silence those traditional voices or close any doors. I think it unwise. Perhaps there is some authenticity hiding there. Through all of this, I am thankful to have my *why* as my beacon. That *why*, no matter where we wind up, will not change … and staying true to it is the path to happiness.

Chapter 5
THE BIG, HARD WORLD

Leaving the military is both a goodbye and a hello. For me, it felt like a rude awakening, a sort of "Welcome to the big, hard world."

I'd like to begin this chapter by putting things into perspective. The U.S. military consists of approximately 1.2 million active duty service-members. The Army, possessing the greatest number of people of all the services, had an active duty end strength of approximately 477,000 in 2019.[1] You can even whittle that down to sub-populations inside the services such as Navy submariners, Marine Raiders or your cohort year group of officer and enlisted — to name only a few. My point is that most of us belong to a small slice of the overall military and only know a relatively small population, even after serving a few decades. It's a small tribe — the few, the proud (in Marine Corps speak). Now consider the population of the United States as a whole, which stands at 329 million residents.[2] You could multiply the entire uniformed military (minus the reserve component) 7 times and fit it into New York City.

---

1   Department of Defense, Defense Manpower Data Center (DMDC), https://www.dmdc.osd.mil/appj/dwp/dwp_reports.jsp

2   United States Census Bureau , https://www.census.gov/programs-surveys/popest/data/data-sets.html

As current or former members of the military, we're a unique minority. An article produced by the Pew Research Center titled, "The Changing Face of America's Veteran Population," highlighted the fact that in the 1980s, 18% of U.S. adults were veterans; today, just 7% of us are veterans. A statistic referenced often by servicemembers (and the media) is "the 1%"[3] — while 7% of Americans are veterans, only 1% of Americans currently wear a uniform. We were and are a microcosm of society at large. The actual number is 0.4% according to Department of Defense Manpower Data[4] and shrinking slightly as the force has experienced manpower cuts in recent years. But wait, I'm not done. Of this 0.4%, many have only served a handful of years. While this population is completely worthy of the title veteran — we all are — most men and women who have served in the Army, Navy, Air Force, Marines or Coast Guard were never truly de-civilianized or "institutionalized" as were those who spent a decade or more. I'll speak to this more in a moment but it is an important distinction. This more junior military population with shorter terms of service has had to shed less of the institutionalism that penetrates deeper the longer you serve.

Indeed, servicemembers coming out of uniform after single-digit years still must adjust to society and many struggle significantly to do so (especially if they have been in combat), but their "civilian membership" hasn't been expired that long. Younger veterans tend to acclimate into civilian life more easily. But being an "outsider" for a very long time (decades or more) changes how you think about the world, and how the world thinks about and relates to you. "The military is a fraction of the total U.S. population" — I remember having heard this often, especially the 1% soundbite, which came up again and again during our years of war. But it all took on a whole new

---

3   Department of Defense, Defense Manpower Data Center (DMDC), https://www.dmdc.osd.mil/appj/dwp/dwp_reports.jsp

4   *Ibid.*

meaning once on the "outside." *Dude! I'm now just a little fish in a big pond!* I felt small. Then I got to thinking about the degree to which *female* servicemembers are even rarer members of society; they represent just 15% of the total active duty force, so they are a *fraction of a fraction* when they jump back into the "big pond" of civilian life. It's all so disorienting and overwhelming at first.

I'd be lying if I said that it didn't bother me to be a small fish in a large pond. *How dare I not be recognized and automatically elevated in status in the general population! Can't you see that big eagle rank on my chest?* Nope. I look like every other guy at a networking conference, at the grocery store, in a job interview or on the beach. No uniform to announce me or call attention to my rank or accomplishments. I felt stripped. Literally.

When I was an Army Colonel, I couldn't travel to most Army bases without being highlighted on a protocol list as a "visiting VIP." I hardly thought of myself as such, but certainly I was amongst a very small population on most Army bases, save for the Pentagon. "Hello, sir," "An honor to meet you, sir," complete with salutes and handshakes. But now that I'm living in a civilian world, I don't *wear* camouflage — I *am* camouflaged. When I walk around downtown Wilmington, North Carolina, a city of over 119,000 people, I am just another schmuck in traffic or a random networker in the corner of a networking event, hoping to be noticed. And in even larger cities, I feel like an even smaller fish. No more do I have that big eagle pinned on my chest for all to notice and pay homage to. "Rank" in this new civilian environment is based on different qualifiers, like your net worth and what chair you occupy in the C-suite. As such, I felt I had to start over on the outside. I kept reminding myself that this was self-inflicted ... that I chose to enter this environment. As uncomfortable as I felt as a new civilian, I had no desire to return to my military-base comfort zone. I knew that I wanted to take on a new adventure in a new place with non-military people, even if it was going to be hard to get started and take a while to fit in.

· ·

As uncomfortable as I felt as a new civilian, I had no desire to return to my military-base comfort zone. I knew that I wanted to take on a new adventure in a new place with non-military people, even if it was going to be hard to get started and take a while to fit in.

· ·

A NEW KIND OF RESUME

While I knew I had made the right decision to retire, I could not ignore the void of recognition I was feeling. Mind you, I'm not a showoff, per se, begging for recognition like those dudes with the big diesel stacks protruding from their 4 x 4 trucks or the obnoxiously loud pipes on their Harley-Davidson motorcycles (sorry guys!). I don't wear a black Iraq and Afghanistan ball cap with all my ribbons on it everywhere I go, though no one would blame me if I did. I'm deeply proud of my service and I have a Bronze Star license plate from the state of North Carolina, but that plate is the only public symbol that indicates my veteran status. I guess I've always lived as a quiet professional. In the military, I had rank. People could tell what I had done and was doing by the patches and ribbons on my uniform. Not much else was needed. On the outside, though, I looked like everyone else … a bit older in fact.

My chosen civilian career path was clear in my mind. I wanted to speak publicly about my leadership journey, be seduced by big companies and help the 99.96%-ers understand veterans. But I found it very hard to communicate what I did. Instant recognition was gone.

Moreover, I felt my service resume was under appreciated. I struggled to communicate my military story.

Me:

"I commanded a brigade of 5,000 soldiers, have three bronze stars and served in Iraq and Afghanistan."

Innocent, well-meaning civilians:

"A brigade … you mean like a fire department?"

"Bronze what? Isn't that a third-place medal in the Olympics?"

"America is still in Afghanistan?"

Blank stares would follow as I made feeble attempts to explain all of this and its importance, especially its value to the business world. Welcome to the big, hard world. I'm a glutton for punishment. Time to apply for a government job on a military base and buy a monster truck?

WHO THE F*** ARE THESE PEOPLE?

I never uttered that out loud but I felt it in several networking events I attended or in meetings with businesses where I was brought in to consult. It was very lonely. Here I was immersed in a new city, far removed from any large military base, surrounded by people unlike me. I walked around in my Colonel's strut, oozing Army values, prepared to take charge in any situation. *No thanks, Colonel.* When I'm in a crowded auditorium, watching someone who never served his or her country speak on stage about leadership or entrepreneurship, I confess my resentment. Perhaps it was jealousy? Salt on my wound. These people woke each morning in peace and safety. Some had not faced hardship, true hardship as I had witnessed in the poor societies of Iraq and Afghanistan. I went forward into the heart of darkness to fight for (and die, if required) the very freedom they were taking for granted right in front of me. I felt like Jack Nicholson in the movie *A Few Good Men*, scoffing at the young lawyers and people in the court room for their lack of a combat resume. Wilmington, like other cities, is certainly supportive of servicemembers (i.e., polite, respectful, throws a parade or two each year) but appears otherwise disinterested. Where I once talked about character, presence, mission command and combat readiness, I now had to converse with people who handed out business cards and spoke net worth and revenue growth.

One of the more difficult things for me to accept was the societal measure of success. With some exceptions, it was dollar-centric and not leadership-based or people-centric. On stage or on front pages of business publications were executives who led a profitable business and whose own compensation packages made them extremely wealthy. It wasn't much more than that. In fairness, there are some very good leaders under the spotlight, but rarely, if ever, do I hear about the retention success in their organization or testimonials from their subordinates or stories of how they inspired their people and overcame a crisis as a team. Those who do take the spotlight as leaders of employee growth and culture are still placed there in large part due to the size of their organization. Stages, podiums and the pages of professional magazines are full of people whose definitions of "leadership" don't match my own.

· ·

Stages, podiums and the pages of professional magazines are full of people whose definitions of "leadership" don't match my own.

· ·

In the Army, with some exceptions, stages, podiums and news coverage were given to leaders via their demonstrated leadership and not the net worth of their company. Those who left a wake of destruction in the Army developed a reputation and many of them were discovered early in their careers and ousted. In Wilmington and similar cities, I'd sit and listen to speeches and mutter to myself, "What does he or she know about leadership, sacrifice and selflessness? Did they practice any of that or just raise money, line their pockets and leave a trail of people-destruction on their journey to the top?" I led people in the most extreme conditions, when the enemy threw us a curveball and everyone was looking to me to guide them. I'd eat last after my soldiers. I'd get behind my boss's guidance and intent with everything I had and serve my people and the team … day and night. I knew leadership. What proof was there that these people did?

I know, I know. You're probably reading this, thinking, "Get control, Campbell! You're now in their world."

Indeed. Of course, I kept my comments and thoughts to myself but it felt truly alien. Though I've gained friendships and assimilated a bit, I still feel — more than three years after retiring from the Army —like there are antennae protruding from my head and I have black pits for eyes. It is because I am institutionalized. A friend told me that it takes a few years to de-institutionalize. I have reached the three-year mark and still very much feel the Army's influence on me. As a younger officer, I remember reading articles written about professionalism. I was a senior Captain and was on the cusp of the commitment to a long Army career. These articles theorized about the point in a soldier's career when he or she became a true professional. The perspective was interesting, especially to me at the 8-year mark of my career. At that point, I had commanded infantry companies and was serving as an Army General's Aide. This was the first time in my career where I could truly see the bigger picture, the Army as an institution. I felt the Army values becoming a part of me and, whereas before I might look up in scorn at Army policy, it began to make more sense. This is not to say that I became a zombie-like follower. I remained critical and still had much more maturing to do but I became a steward of the Army values and all we stood for, more so than I had before. I saw the Army from a wider lens. This stewardship, the influence and allure of the Army values, the mission and our culture sank deeper into me with each passing year. While I cherished (and still do) these values and the Army code, in an instant I was thrust into the big, hard world.

Holding On, Letting Go and Embracing a New Normal

Sebastian Junger's book, *Tribe: On Homecoming and Belonging,* was released the same year I retired from the Army and its perspectives really helped me understand what I was going through. In fact, I have turned to my tabbed and highlighted copy several times as I wrestle with my feelings. In his book, Junger strikes at the core of what veterans experience when we return home from combat or, in the case of those of us making the final military/civilian transition, step outside the walls of our profession after a long career. At first, we are enamored by and reminded of all the riches of our nation. The things we became accustomed to and missed are immediately replaced. What follows shortly is the utter lack of community or tribe and self-lessness in society (for those of us who believe in "selfless service" as a core value, this is jarring). Junger highlights problems like depression and anxiety, which are prevalent in affluent societies like ours. He talks about dishonesty — punishable by death in tribal societies, and by loss of rank, pay or by discharge under the uniformed code for servicemembers — yet overlooked in modern ones like the one servicemembers come home to in the United States.

. . . .

Selfishness was probably the most foreign characteristic I found when immersing myself in modern civilian society. I encountered too many people who would chase a buck at the cost of a person's wellbeing, and who would place an organization above its people and serve themselves instead of their community or others around them.

. . . .

Selfishness was probably the most foreign characteristic I found when immersing myself in modern civilian society. I encountered too many people who would chase a buck at the cost of a person's wellbeing, and who would place an organization above its people and serve themselves instead of their community or others around them. There were too many occasions when I witnessed people implying or literally asking, "What's in it for me?" This was my biggest WTF. Again, Junger came to my aid, if only to put into words what I was feeling:

> "A society that doesn't offer its members the chance to act selflessly isn't a society in any tribal sense of the word; it's just a political entity that, lacking enemies, will probably fall apart on its own. Soldiers experience this tribal thinking at war, but when they come home they realize that the tribe they were actually fighting for was their unit. It makes absolutely no sense to make sacrifices for a group that itself isn't willing to make sacrifices for you."[5]

Selfless service, my most favored Army value, ran through my veins. Sure, I wanted my piece of the pie; I had dreams that required funding. But I know I felt a great sense of fulfillment when I was able to use my years of experience to help another person, and that sense of fulfillment has always gone way beyond a paycheck. In fairness to

---

5   Sebastian Junger, *Tribe: On Homecoming and Belonging*, Twelve, 2016, p. 110.

all the civilians I started encountering after my military retirement, there were several who gave of themselves and their riches to help others. I did find many members of society, especially the younger generations, who believed in making the world a better place and who were trying to identify their roles in that quest. I believe it was the executive-level business environment I was now a part of where I met this tone of selfishness. I didn't want to be like the rest of the guys. "Pay it forward" was and will always be part of my philosophy in this new world. I wondered if it would come full circle. And I hoped.

So, what now Campbell? Being an optimistic person, I didn't care to live the remainder of my days in civilian land with a chip on my shoulder. Resentment and jealousy were products of my ego, which needed to be tamed, now more than ever. I had to realize that society would not change to accommodate me; I had to change to align to society, or at least find a way to fit in. Let me be clear: It was not time for me to shed all that I stood for and knew to be important. Neither did I want to dismiss or disavow decades of great memories and honed leadership skills. Quite the opposite. I still have all my military bling — colored flags, plaques expressing gratitude for my leadership and service in numerous units and a large military challenge coin collection. I still use all the military lingo around my house and with the businesses for which I consult. I love it and will hold on to it as long as I can. Reach out to me in 10 years. Perhaps it will have faded a bit. But I hope not.

When returning from Afghanistan in the spring of 2010 after a hard year of fighting during the surge, my commander introduced a phrase that wound up getting printed on banners and touted in the narrative of our redeployment briefings. "Return to Normal." It meant that while each of us had changed through our experiences fighting together, we were returning to a society that had not. It was those of us coming back from deployment who needed to return to the normal ways of life — the life we left behind. In combat, we wore body armor, traveled in armored vehicles and practiced near-martial law with complete authority to go anywhere, answering to almost no one. We were the supreme rulers of our environment. In combat, we experienced hardship and sacrificed our freedoms while, back at home, the general population, even that of our military bases, lived in peace. The phrase "return to normal" was aimed at the behaviors of entitlement and resentment displayed by many servicemembers returning from war. A simple ID

Rob and Leslie reuniting after 12 arduous months of combat in Afghanistan — Rob's second combat deployment.

and vehicle check at the main gate of post or an attitude from a bad employee at a store or a display of selfishness or laziness might set off a freshly returned war veteran. We felt a huge sense of entitlement, as if society owed us something upon our return. These beliefs turned into behaviors like yelling profanity or even physical harm of an innocent military policeman or store clerk. My boss was trying to head that off before it manifested. His point: it was *us* who needed to assimilate back to society. Society would not roll out the red carpet for us and give us a pass for our combat service. They would not understand what it was we went through and, to an extent, they didn't really need to. Our lives forward in combat were anything but normal but we were home now and it was time to return to normal.

It occurred to me, after I retired, that the same philosophy needed to apply to my post-military return to society — a society I left in 1990 when I went on active duty. I needed to bottle up my resentment and place it far away. I decided to learn the language of business. I took free business courses as I was starting up my own business and I needed to hear from the experts in this new space. I would network like crazy, softening my language and translating "brigade" to "organization" and "commander" to "CEO." I would bottle up my resentment, leave it in the trunk and enter networking events with a smile and a stack of business cards. I had no issue as an Army commander if a subordinate developed an idea I could learn from. Indeed, I had soldiers, far younger than I, who knew modern warfare tactics better than I ... and I had no issue with it. In fact, I'd celebrate their knowledge and learn from it. In my new world, I would need to do the same. I'd listen to speeches and clap as loud as the others, then try to meet with the speakers to learn how they did what they did. I'd think about what military experience I could draw from to help others be more selfless. Where I found the money grabber with dollar signs in his or her eyes, I'd kindly slip away. I made a conscious effort to find those people who I believed wanted to do right by their people and I would hang with them. I came to grips with the fact that society would not hand me a CEO position and a large staff just because I commanded on a scale they had not. I admitted to myself what I was lacking. I possessed leadership and operational prowess but I was lacking business acumen. I had to confess to myself that I had much to learn in this world I had not lived in. These "f***ing people," young and old, had much to teach me and, as much as I helped them as a consultant and a leader, I became *their* student in this new, big, hard world.

· ·

I possessed leadership and operational prowess but I was lacking business acumen.

· ·

Chapter 6
THE JOB SWAMP

"I really *enjoyed* my job search and interview experience ..." said no person — ever! Because the job search is really a *job swamp*, and most people avoid swamps. Swamps are incredibly hard to navigate through. You can't see beyond the nasty surface, so you don't know what to expect with each step. Swamps are messy, smelly and full of ugly creatures. Yeah, that's pretty much the job environment in the civilian world.

I wish I could put a better face on it, but after what my wife and I experienced, nope! As I shared with you in the opening chapters of this book, I didn't embark on a feverish job search when I first left the Army. I didn't fill out hundreds of applications, nor did I seek dozens of interviews. I did, however, wade far enough into the job swamp to be able to offer some perspective and advice to you now. Indeed, my time working with the networking company I engaged did prepare me well for the experience. I did all the standard things most job seekers do. I sat in front of a computer screen, perusing the most popular job sites, searching for job titles, studying the job descriptions and attempt to determine salary that might be offered for each available position. I guess these were the first gates I needed to get through before navigating through painful job applications. In addition to this basic research about the job positions, I would also look where those positions were housed; I looked at company size, location and checked to see if there were any veterans serving in that organization using my LinkedIn search. On LinkedIn, I could type in the company name, then follow the link that read, *"See all [X number] employees on LinkedIn."* There, I could search to see who among them might be veterans. A veteran could vouch for a few things that I considered important. Was the company a good one to work for and did it have a good culture, a clear vision and an admirable set of values? Would I be happy there, what would my chances for advancement be and could the veteran connect me with the hiring authority to get me past the heavily defended entry control point called HR?

I knew some transitioning Vets who went straight for salary, meaning they believed they could do just about anything (as I did) but considered salary to be foremost in their criteria. All the maneuvering and sleuthing in the job search — the online job boards, the applications, the contrived networking — felt phony to me. I filled in the blocks of online job applications mixed with a lack of confidence and deep reservation. Of course, I could always refuse a job if it didn't feel right, so no damage done, right? The thing that bothered me most, perhaps, about the job search process was my commitment of time to something that did not feel authentic to me.

Man, it ain't like it used to be! Before I left the civilian world in 1990 and entered through the iron gates of the military, job hunting was about filling out a paper application and pestering a manager frequently to prove that I wanted the job. I was good at this. I scored a bunch of jobs as a young adult by showing a potential boss that "I was their man." There wasn't a "network" in the sense that there is today. Of course, who you knew and who could vouch for you with a potential employer was important but it really boiled down to knocking on the door, shaking a hand and taking it from there. Today, the process is almost completely virtual. In fact, I filled out many an application or conducted a phone interview still wearing my gym clothes, unshaven, not having brushed my teeth. I spent more time on the phone interviewing with people instead of sitting across from their desk or in front of a panel of people. It felt foreign and impersonal. I was confident that if I could get to a conversation, especially in person, I stood a very good chance of landing the job. Gone are the days when looking for a job in town or in the closest city within commuting range was the norm. Now, job candidates competed in an impersonal cattle call against people sometimes thousands of miles away. Welcome back to the world, Campbell.

VETERAN-FRIENDLY BUT NOT VETERAN-READY

"Thank you for your service!" Yeah, yeah, yeah. It usually feels like lip service, though I know it generally comes from a place of kindness. I do feel very touched by that phrase, even as the distance between my military service increases. But the friendliness and admiration employers have for us military types, while genuine, typically lives on the surface but doesn't go very deep. Entering the job swamp after separating from the Army, I expected to be in high demand for leadership opportunities. I had heard from others, throughout my career and especially at times when I considered separating, that the opportunities for me in Corporate America were endless. It was comforting to believe this was true, especially as I gained seniority, experience and advanced my education. I expected that corporations would be drooling and fighting over me right out of the gate. "What?! Rob Campbell is available? We want him ... You can't have him." But what I heard instead was silence. That's right, Mr. In High Demand didn't get any knocks on the door or phone calls. Nobody came running to take advantage of my skills and experience. I was unaccustomed to the anonymity in which I found myself.

Shortly after retirement from the Army, I applied to be the executive director for human resources at a local community college. It certainly was not a dream job or the reason I retired, but I thought it might be a good step into academia, a place I was interested to explore. I believed that I could break into the community college leadership ranks, form a strong HR team and take the organization to new heights. I imagined the role could prove to be fulfilling and it appeared aligned with my passion. I received an email thanking me for applying but notifying me that I was not considered. I was honestly shocked and humbled not to be even considered. After speaking with an employee of the college, I learned that in order to be considered for an HR leadership position there, I would need to be a Society for Human Resource Management Certified Professional (i.e., to be SHRM-CP certified). I'll never know for sure, but I suspect that my lack of this certification may have disqualified me. This was a rude awakening. I had led the #1 brigade in the Army for human resource performance. We led our division in retention. I wrote a damned book on personal leadership! I can't imagine a problem that I would not be able to handle in this community college. But it didn't matter. I had taken a swing and it was a miss; I'd struck out.

I've used this true story numerous times when explaining my frustration with the civilian job market. It speaks to what author Bob Woodward dubbed as an epidemic of disconnection between society writ large and the 0.4% of U.S. citizens who serve in the military.[1] It speaks to a comparison a friend made. Are businesses just veteran-friendly or are they truly veteran-ready? Veteran-friendly requires only a "thank you for your service." Veteran-ready, on the other hand, requires a business to replicate many of the aspects of military life, like leadership, worth, purpose, cause, culture and values, to name only a few. It requires businesses to understand the

---

1   https://invictusfoundation.org/2011/04/u-s-society-disconnected-from-its-warriors-insightful-and-thought-provoking-article/

true value of the word *veteran* and all that the military experience brings. My time working inside of several businesses — involved in their hiring process as well as my numerous conversations with transitioned veterans — highlighted a few things for me. Often, employers will view veterans competing for the same job on an equal plane. For instance, a Navy supply clerk with four years and a Marine Captain of eight years who commanded a company — the two of whom have vastly different skills and experience — could be seen as equals in a business. Indeed, the supply clerk might be the better fit or vice versa but the lack of perspective in veteran vetting spoils the job search. I've seen many businesses default to hiring people they are familiar with, such as those who attended the same college as the hiring manager, those who hold the same kind of college degree or those who grew up near them. When hiring civilians or veterans, thinking all people are equal among certain groups (i.e., a Midwesterner is a Midwesterner, a Kappa Phi is a Kappa Phi, a veteran is a veteran) sells everyone short, including the employer.

Are businesses just veteran-friendly or are they truly veteran-ready?

I've even known a few transitioning servicemembers who didn't want to mention their years of military service on their resume or check the "veteran" box on a job application. Many HR professionals simply cannot understand what a servicemember did and how it might apply to their company. We have tackled tasks far outside our "job description" in our years, even in the throes of combat zones. But even with the best MOS translation for your skills and a "civilianized" resume, communicating the value of that specialized, battle-tested experience — especially on paper — to a hiring agent is a steep mountain to climb. Lastly, but not least, the level of responsibility that gets placed on the shoulders of servicemembers when they're in uniform is immense compared to what I have seen inside modern businesses. A 21-year-old Airman leading a squad of six people is charged with the health and welfare of his or her people ... as well as sometimes hundreds of thousands of dollars of equipment. That same Airman, in a civilian setting, is likely to be charged (and trusted with) very little based on age alone. I've spoken to dozens of veterans, junior and senior alike, during my transition years and the level of responsibility and authority they enjoy in a civilian company pales in comparison to what they had in the military. This is a source of frustration for them and a strike at their self-esteem.

In the spring of 2017, about six months after my official Army retirement ceremony, I took a job at a company for which I had done some consulting. The owner wanted me to serve as his vice president and help strengthen his team and grow his business. He had lofty goals but did not lead well. Like the HR position at the community college, I saw a glimmer of hope in this VP opportunity; I hoped it would be an opportunity to lead and grow people and establish some organizational structure, thus taking this business to new heights. I saw a challenge and I wanted to address it head on. I agreed to join him full time and bring my consulting business to a halt. The job lasted exactly one week. It was the worst on-boarding I have ever experienced. Not one person made an effort to welcome me and help me get established. Doors were closed to the parts of the business I really needed to see. Even my gentle prodding did not work. It started badly and then all came crashing down over a violation in character. I was witness to an inappropriate joke loaded with sexual innuendos; I confronted it immediately but found myself alone in my stance. A red line was crossed and, in an instant, my future with that organization was over.

I was angered, saddened and embarrassed that I hadn't foreseen this lack of character and values. Better yet would have been identifying it before I took the job and realizing that I could not fix it. Like any situation, I pulled the lessons and positives from it. The experience allowed me to examine a business (even if only briefly) and create some concepts and methodologies I could use elsewhere. It hardened me a bit. I became more acutely aware of the warning signs in a company and less alarmed perhaps at the lack of professionalism and obedience to values in a non-military private organization. The company was not ready for this seasoned military leader.

So, as it turned out, I was headed back to the swamp (or back to building my consulting business, or a little bit of both). Here comes my ego again, but I thought ... *"How dare a company not immediately respect my rank and experience? People stood up for me when I entered the room only a few short years ago! How dare they think I must enter their organization at a middle-management level, answering to someone who couldn't lead a hungry squad to a snack bar! I'm a large-organization leader who commands respect and possesses massive authority and responsibility! What do you know about leadership? What danger or hardship have you ever faced?"*

Rob and Leslie vacationing with family in Hilton Head, SC. (He swears he didn't buy her that shirt!)

Settle down, Campbell. Fortunately, a friend helped me put things into perspective. And I think this is an important point for any transitioning senior servicemember, so listen up. In the military, we would never allow a 50-year-old experienced executive with a great resume but zero military experience to command servicemembers on day 1. Someone like that would have to enter at a lower level in the military organization and prove their worth, credibility and talents. Why then should I expect a company, which does not enjoy the security of its existence under a large Department of Defense budget, to place complete trust in me to serve effectively at its most senior levels? Moreover, in the military, we were *given* our employees and someone else paid them and provided their benefits. While we were certainly measured by our contributions to our organizations, we did not have a dollar sign attached to us like you find in a business. Each employee is an expense for a business owner. In fact, staffing is the most expensive part of running a business. If you as an individual are not contributing to revenue gains, you are a liability and not an asset. In the military, we had depth in our organizations. A colonel or captain who gave 70% might be penalized by not being selected for a command but he or she would still be paid the same and the organization would survive. In a civilian-run business, the 70% colonel or captain would be fired.

OFF THE ARMY BASE AND INTO THE FRAY: LESLIE WADES INTO THE SWAMP TOO

I was not alone in the experience of feeling "out of my element" in the job swamp. Leslie ventured into the swamp as well. Once we settled on a home (a beach house on Topsail Island, NC), she began her job search. Her Army spouse prowess came in handy as she ventured into new territory yet she went about this search with the same 1980s high school "find a job" experience that I had prior to us attending college and then beginning our Army journey. The job search experience for her was dismal. I cannot give it a better description than that. Leslie had a teaching degree but had not taught since 2006 when we were stationed in North Carolina. She applied to several schools and, using the 1990s approach, knocked on a few doors. It was mid-summer so she mostly encountered administrators holding down the fort while the faculty was off on break. She was able to meet or speak on the phone with a couple of principals and some conversations were promising but nothing materialized. She was able to sit through a few interviews, which were nerve-racking and a bit dry. Most troubling was the dead silence that inevitably followed each of these encounters.

Leslie did finally land a job as the coordinator for an afterschool program. Following her interview there, as was the trend, she heard nothing. School was about to begin, so she grew understandably nervous that her teaching career may have ended for good. She contacted the principal and learned that she was, in fact, hired and would start the following week. "*Gee, thanks for the heads up!*" Leslie would experience an on-boarding process much like the one I'd just experienced at the "VP for a week" debacle. While there were no gross violations of ethics or integrity afoot at her new job, she felt alien and under-appreciated in the organization. In keeping with her never-quit attitude, she rode out the year and certified the program ahead of schedule (and to the delight of district inspectors). Institutionalized as I was, she had a difficult time existing in an organization quite the opposite from what we had experienced in the military. Leslie would come home each day disheveled. I don't recall her ever smiling or bringing home great news, save for the program certification. The school was amazed at her ability to get the program certified like she did and impressed by her creativity, innovative development programs and reputation amongst the parents. But their appreciation and support came too late. After a year surrounded by selfishness, poor leadership, and an almost complete lack of belonging and community, she bid that job farewell.

FROM COLONEL TO CONSULTANT

At this point in my transition to an encore career, I was all-in on a future as a consultant. While I didn't pursue jobs, I certainly pursued business. I wanted businesses to pay me for my decades of leadership experience and my analysis, counsel and coaching. Similar to applying for a job, I had to get through a few obstacles. The first and most difficult (still is) was the stigma of being a veteran. Perhaps stigma is too strong a word but I'm talking about the notion that many civilians have about us, like we are all PTSD ticking time-bombs or abrasive "take the hill" leaders who would take a wrecking ball to

Rob addressing the troops while commanding the 1st Brigade, 101st Airborne Division (Fort Campbell, KY, 2014).

their organization. I felt a ton of respect and admiration, but with that I could also sense misunderstanding and doubt.

Consider the two environments — the U.S. military vs. Corporate America. In the U.S. military, we serve in a time-honored profession steeped in tradition, values and ethics, where leadership is everything. We're guided in our military careers by shared values like selfless service, duty, honor and personal courage. Our successes are marked by the units we led and how they performed, our reputations and leadership abilities. Our credentials are our servicemembers and their loving families. In a business, on the other hand, success is centered around money and market share. Indeed, there are numerous businesses out there, many in the non-profit sector, which resemble the inspirational cause and mission we dedicated our lives to. And there are good leaders in businesses who wake each morning wanting to do right by their people. The challenge is the almighty dollar, which can cause business leaders to cast aside good leadership and care of people, including customers.

Leadership came naturally to me — both leading and talking about leading and leader development. And as members of the armed forces, we were groomed as leaders at every step of our careers. We became students of leadership and constant practitioners. This is *not* the culture or commitment in most businesses. There is no "Career Course" or "Command and Staff College" in a business, though there may be sporadic and short-term professional development workshops, mentorship or coaching programs. Leaders in civilian businesses are chosen because they display some perceived leadership traits or because they demonstrate some intelligence, maturity, deep functional or industry expertise, and/or company loyalty. That is about the extent of it. A year or so after leaving the Army, I realized I would need to ease my way into a business, using caution not to ruffle any feathers with my military speak or formal concepts of leadership.

LOOKING BACK ...

At the time of publication of this book, I was entering my fourth year as a civilian and settling comfortably into my encore career as a leadership consultant and transition advisor. When I reflect on the job swamp and how I handled it back in 2016 and 2017, I realize that if I had it to do all over again, I would alter my approach at bit. In many cases, I should have boxed up my ego and left it in the car or closet. I'm a humble person by nature but I found myself getting resentful and defensive. I'm sure I lost a few opportunities because of it. Of course, passion over paycheck should have dominated my job search or prevented me from conducting a job search at all. I confess the rejections were hard to take. I didn't spin into a period of depression but the "no thank you's" were a bitter pill to swallow. I don't live with a ton of regret about the time and money I spent on the networking company, though, because I put some of the things they taught me into practice. In fact, I still do as I continue to network.

Network. If there is one word I would share with any transitioning servicemember, it is network. Looking back, I can trace all my opportunities to a network. My first consulting client came from a business mentor of mine. I saw him speak at a center for entrepreneurship and I walked up to meet him after. We had coffee and spent most of the time talking about modern warfare. He was curious about our wars and was uneducated about them. He, like me, was eager to learn so I gave him the unclassified version over coffee. He connected me with my first client and it took off from there. *Network.* It's a verb and a noun; you must do it, and have one. Starting over, I would rely more on the network than an online application. In my journey, I learned to reverse the conversation. I offered my experience, asked to learn about what another person was doing, what pain points they were experiencing and how I could help. I usually left out any specific requests I had or money or doors I wanted open. That could come in a subsequent conversation. Of course, if they opened the door to discussions of money or work, I would walk through it, but it was never my intent going in. All my job offers and consulting clients came through a network of people I met, none through an online form.

The job swamp taught me something I'd like to now teach you: Do not expect to be offered the same level of responsibility and authority on the outside. For a period of time, even the highest-ranking military leaders, if they try to break into the civilian workforce, will find themselves earning their way back up — up the corporate ladder instead of the rank and file. Do your best to understand the realities of this and don't let your ego get in the way. I should have listened to my friend Tim and toned it down. I was proud of what I did and I wanted to flaunt it, I guess. I hope you will learn from my experience. Be grateful for the time someone is giving you. While we were busy in the military, we were paid regardless. In the big, hard world, time is money. Literally. I use this humble philosophy in my business practice today and suggest it for you. In my business, I coach and consult for people I would not in the Army. Most of the work I do, I could have easily delegated to a more junior leader while in uniform. In this new life and career, I can still make big difference and it's fulfilling. I don't need 5,000 men and women standing in front of me. Five is just fine. I find that once I start speaking and can offer solutions to problems that are bothering my audiences or clients, they gain a greater understanding and appreciation for what I bring. And I have learned from them too. I find fascination in what they wrestle with, how they do their jobs in the modern world, how they outsource tasks to electronic business applications and handle large task lists with little, if any, supporting people. From the job interview to the consulting client, I've become their student, thankful for their time and interest and their money, fascinated by the industries in which they thrive.

In this new life and career, I can still make big difference and it's fulfilling. I don't need 5,000 men and women standing in front of me. Five is just fine.

Chapter 7
FREE TO MAKE BOLD MOVES

Back when I was busy being a soldier, I thought little about my post-military life. Sure, I periodically mused about what I wanted to do and what needed to be done to experience a successful transition and be happy "on the other side," but that thinking and planning was something I didn't do to the extent that I should have. And in fairness, most of us in the military don't give the "encore life and career" sufficient thought because we are consumed by the demands of our *current* jobs and lives. I was no different from the uniformed crowd, even though I had 27 years to plan my exit. Just like waiting on an official set of orders before you call schools and conduct hard inquiries about housing each time we PCS'd, I would not do much but ponder the journey until the Army blessed off on my retirement with an official document.

But once the winter of 2015 rolled around and the decision was made and the approval was received, I was free to make some bold moves. For the first time, I could communicate with assurance that I would be available wherever needed upon the date of my retirement. I could plan vacations, commit to being at family reunions or other special occasions. I could think about new hobbies and new activities and new ways of living.

You have now read approximately half of this book, I'd like to now give you a peek at the current state of my life and career, sharing the highlights of the events and outline the steps I took in sequence. Forgive me for a bit of purposeful repetition, where I remind you exactly what I did, when and why. It's my hope that my journey — what went well and what didn't — will be instructive and supportive to you. The journey is still underway and, I as I type these words, I cannot say for sure what I'll be doing when this book hits the shelves (though it looks like I'll still be in COVID-19 quarantine along with the rest of the world, learning to provide more of my consulting services via video and virtual interactions). No matter what the future holds for me, my family and my career, I can promise you that I will always be diligent in my pursuit of authenticity, purpose and passion.

· ·

I will always be diligent in my pursuit of authenticity, purpose and passion.

· ·

FACEBOOK AND LINKEDIN AND TWITTER, OH MY!

Retirement orders in hand and looking ahead to 2016 — my final months in the Army — my first discretionary act was to get out of my foxhole and enter the social networking arena. While I did not fully grasp the power of networking, I knew enough to see the value of social networks. My military email account would soon be gone, as would the opportunity to cross paths with several of my military buddies as we all navigated our careers. I would proudly joke with social media junkie members of my family that I was not up on "Linked Book" or "Face-a-gram." The joke was over. I opened a LinkedIn account and a Facebook profile. I would later experiment with Instagram and Twitter but I found that LinkedIn would be my primary place for professional networking. I felt like the old man you see in commercials with some young, bearded, tattooed punk showing him how to leverage the internet at the speed of light. I would do some studying, reading and rely on family members to help me become a social network Jedi.

As of 2020, I haven't achieved Jedi status yet and probably never will but social media has been hugely effective for me, especially in my quest to enter the big, hard world. I could feel myself creeping toward the abyss of my post-military life with each "post," "friend" and "connection." Of course, I knew a bunch of military folks, so I connected with them first to build my network, but I knew this would not be sufficient. I would need to connect with executives in companies across a range of industries to showcase Rob Campbell, former military leader and overall leadership expert. I would need to connect with those who were far younger than I but with different experiences and qualifications that I could learn from. As of this writing, I'm rapidly approaching 19,000 connections on LinkedIn. It's only a number, of course, but it gives me a large possible audience to whom I can broadcast each video, article, insight, offer or announcement.

I then proceeded to reach out to those who went before me, especially retired colonels. I knew several officers who had retired before I had, and I wanted to hear about their experience. They would understand, like no other, what I was going through and what I would soon experience. I asked them questions aligned with my philosophies and theories about pay, what they found to be the most difficult part of the transition, if they "took a knee" or launched an encore career, and how they approached disability. I asked about their experience in the modern workplace. We talked about a variety of things, like taxes, graduate-level studies and physical training (PT). These were beneficial conversations — priceless, game-changing conversations — and I took copious notes, which I still have and refer to from time to time.

PROFESSIONAL NETWORKING AND THE DREADED JOB SEARCH

At the beginning of my transition (a period of time from about January 2016 to August 2016, the interval between making my plans to retire official and the time I actually separated from service), I believed I would take another job after leaving the Army. So I spent a lot of time thinking about and imagining what it would be. As I first mentioned in Chapter 3, I began to search for jobs on websites like Glassdoor.com. I had no idea what kind of money I could demand. I also felt that I would need to enter an organization as a leader. Hell, I thought of myself as a CEO and could envision myself assuming "command" of a company, learning its products or services and leading it to excellence. My ego was flaring. In addition to career search sites, I typed in "executive jobs." This brought me to networking agencies that served business executives in search of positions that would pay healthy six-figure salaries. That sounded like me, so I connected with one of the executive networking firms and became their client. I thought they could help me cross the military/civilian career divide and find something lucrative. I always had my passion in the back of my mind, meaning I would know a right fit when I found it, but I confess the dollar signs were attractive. Money, strange as this will sound to civilians, was a bit foreign to me. Certainly, I understood what level of income I would need to sustain our lifestyle but the military spoiled me, taking the mystery out of pay. I knew what I was going to make. There was no negotiating salary and compensation. The money was pretty good and we lived within our pay. Now, I had no idea how to describe to someone what I believed I was worth. I knew it was a healthy sum, but still felt unprepared to describe what I thought it should be.

I had no idea how to describe to someone what I believed I was worth.

So began my executive networking experience. I had a talented coach who guided me through conversations and connected me with executives in the private sector. This agency helped me create a solid resume, one I still use today. I watched a series of videos and completed some surveys about what industry I might like to work in. Here again, I struggled. I would be happy leading a group of people in a packaging plant, healthcare organization or a tech company. It was a simple as that. My coach tried to steer me toward the defense industry but I felt sure that wasn't where I wanted to be. This said, I didn't want to close any doors (at least not just yet). In the end, it would come down to what job a company wanted me to do, what compensation they offered, and how it might align with my purpose and passions.

I learned quite a bit on this journey. And I became a great networker. I was always a gifted conversationalist and an extrovert, so I could easily reach out in the blind and connect with an executive to learn more about what they did and seek their feedback on where they would place me in their industry. With each conversation I had, I learned more about what an executive experienced in his or her field. They might share a few contacts for me to pursue and politely offer to stay in touch. None of my phone conversations ended in a job offer but I knew it would come eventually. It took a lot of patience and daily management of my ego.

Early in my networking journey, just prior to my final departure from Colorado, I connected with an Army buddy of mine who had sepa-rated only a few years ahead of me. Our conversations centered on our decisions to retire. Truthfully, we were feeding our egos, bashing the Army and justifying our decisions to move on. The egotistical part of our conversations grew old but I did appreciate our discussions about purpose and passion. I would meet with him frequently over beer and we'd cover new ground. He was on a fulfilling journey, one which he created and I admired that. I also admired his approach following his retirement, as he deliberately took some time off. He was "smoked," as we would say, or fresh off the treadmill ... having completed an arduous and lengthy stint in the Army, and he wanted time to think and reflect before taking the next step. The more we would talk, the more this idea became attractive to me.

Of course, this approach — the idea of taking a sort of "gap year" between my military service and my encore career —was very counter to the networking path I was traveling. It was hard to admit it, but I was headed down the wrong path. Thankfully, I had recently trained myself to listen to my true inner voice. It was time to pull off the highway. I contacted my executive networking coach and told her to pump the brakes. While I desired to network, I wanted to decrease the pace, focus on my transition, place geography over job and take my own time to package up an amazing career and ponder my future. As it would end up, I never really took an executive position as a result of my networking company. Perhaps someday I will.

· ·

While I desired to network, I wanted to decrease the pace, focus on my transition, place geography over job and take my own time to package up an amazing career and ponder my future.

· ·

2016: THE FINAL MONTHS BEFORE SEPARATING

Spring 2016 came on fast, and with it came Louden's high school graduation. His graduation ceremony marked the end of the K-12 public-school chapter of our lives. No more would schools inform or dictate where we would live. (And, pretty soon, neither would the Army!) Voting geography over job, we chose to settle along the North Carolina coast as soon as my military service was behind us. So, as it turned out, Colorado — beautiful and lovely as it was —would soon enter the Campbell family history books ... as so many other great places had. We decided to pack up our stuff and head east. Robbie, finishing his college years, would remain in Utah while Leslie and Louden would preposition themselves on the east coast. I would wrap up my duties at NORTHCOM, hyper-focus on an important transition and reunite with my family once again. Leslie spent some time with her parents in Pennsylvania and our youngest, Louden, visited some friends from a previous high school. I found a spot to spread out an air mattress and served my last "hardship tour" in my final days in uniform. I would follow the prescribed path toward retirement, listening attentively to all the dedicated civilians who assisted me with each step. I was able to hand the reins off to my deputy and totally focus on my transition.

The final weeks were strange. I kept normal hours, sprinkled with transition appointments, to help my headquarters prepare for and conduct a major exercise before handing off the reins to my deputy to spend my final weeks transitioning. I felt very alone. For one, I had never really connected, on a social level, to the unit I had joined in Colorado. While I had formed some friendships, they were all with people I would leave behind. My retirement appointments were just me and a manila folder. I'd grab lunch or FaceTime with my wife and think about the future, but I felt most of the big decisions were made. We knew where we were headed (in fact, Leslie and Louden were already there), Leslie would find a job to help us transition, I would get our house assembled and prepare myself for the next step, and Louden would begin his college journey at the local community college so we could gain residency and he could discover his own path. By the fall Robbie, would transition into a career in Salt Lake

City, Utah, where he would remain until he and Meggie moved to Germany in October of 2018.

One day, I found myself feeling emotional, reflecting on all that we had been through as a family and the amazing journey the Army allowed me (and us!) to take. My last day in my Army combat uniform lacked any kind of pomp and circumstance. I arrived at the Fort Carson, Colorado, Transition Center for my early and final appointments. There I signed my leave form and received my ever-important Certificate of Release or Discharge from Active Duty (also known simply as the DD214). On my last transition station, I was handed a box containing my retirement pin, a folded flag and a certificate. I don't recall much about the woman who handed me these parting gifts, aside from her being very sweet and congratulatory. It was a nice moment yet void of any celebration. With that box and a handful of important papers, I walked outside alone, greeted by the burning August sun of Colorado. I called my wife, told her I loved her and said, "We did it!" The moment was not necessarily liberating, like being freed from prison might be, but I did experience a mix of nostalgia, sadness, excitement and fear. Of course, this was only the start of my remaining or terminal leave period. I would not officially be off the Army's books until October but the last chapter, our Colorado assignment, was over. The true end was in sight. No longer would I be accounted for as I had been every day and every hour of my 27 years, 5 months and 7 days in the Army. On the other hand, no longer would I be under the care of the military. I was on my own and, as the song says, "The Army went rolling along." This time, it went rolling along without me.

TAKING SOME TIME OFF

Hmmm. To do what? Though not yet in possession of a hammock, I did have my favorite pillow, the solitaire app on my phone and a few good books downloaded. I was not one of those who needed to "get out of the house" and head off to an office each day. This "take time and reflect" philosophy opened new doors for me. I had considered hiking the Appalachian Trail from start to finish. I also considered — very seriously — writing, politics, speaking and even cooking and learning a second language. This next mission was mine to decide. As you know, we ended up buying a home at the beach in North Carolina. There, I took charge of landscaping, unpacking and parting with some unwanted furniture and household goods. Boxes, packing tape, shovels and rakes became my new soldiers. We got along just fine.

· ·

I had considered hiking the Appalachian Trail from start to finish. I also considered — very seriously — writing, politics, speaking and even cooking and learning a second language. This next mission was mine to decide.

· ·

Leslie found a job at a middle school, leading the afterschool program. It would help us through the transition but we never saw it as something long term. Her new schedule and my time of reflection meant a role reversal in our marriage. As for Louden, he would adjust to our new surroundings, but it would not be permanent for him. In a year, he would be off to college. Louden only knew life in the military. He had traveled the journey with us to the very end and on his own after his brother Robbie left home for school in 2012. Louden attended three different high schools, so he was a champion when it came to adjusting. He had made some very close high school friends especially at Fort Campbell where he attended the on-post high school for his sophomore and junior year. The beach, however, would be different.

There were many vacation homes on the island and while Leslie and I embraced the peace of it, Louden would be void of a new local posse of friends. He soldiered on, as he always did. It was the beach, after all, and Louden embraced it, catching some rays, learning to surf and finding employment at one of the local restaurants. At year's end, he would transfer to the University of North Carolina, Asheville, where he remains today. His year on the island was productive but, like his brother, he was ready to be on his own.

Rob with two people he loves dearly — his in-laws, Conrad and Theresa Hamp (Topsail Island, NC, 2017).

I cooked and cleaned. It gave me a new appreciation for all Leslie had done all these years, especially the cooking. With grace, she navigated the kitchen pot to pot, altering recipes and making up dishes on the fly, all the while conversing with me and catching up on our busy day. The result, a phenomenal meal. I, on the other hand, was a caveman in the kitchen. I didn't possess her grace and talent. Sticking to rigid timelines and recipe instructions, I'd produce the family dinner. If we were lucky, it might be good enough for leftovers. I did eventually pull off some very tasty dishes and, I admit, learning to cook was fun. But I didn't then and don't now have chef on my "passion list." I'll leave it at that.

Aside from my household focus, I did dabble in some writing. I wrote a short editorial about how grateful I was to serve. I submitted a piece or two on terrorism and modern warfare but neither got far. I did fill out a few job applications for positions nearby but they were so insignificant I don't recall what the positions were. I had a mortgage now, and soon would have to bring in some income above my retired pay to support my family. I also started attending networking events and meeting with business leaders, practicing what my networking coach taught me. I even returned to regular coaching sessions and executive phone conversations, albeit at a deliberate pace ... but none of it felt real. My inner voice grew louder. That October, I hosted my retirement ceremony where we reconnected with old friends and our family. It was a wonderful celebration. We spent Thanksgiving and Christmas with family, free from the tug of the military. It felt wonderful.

MAYBE I WANT TO BE AN AUTHOR WHEN I GROW UP

Then, in January, an Army buddy of mine offered me a spot at an entrepreneur's conference in Whistler, British Columbia. There I was able to connect with young entrepreneurs, none of whom had served in the military but all of whom had enjoyed success in their own businesses. Each day, we would mastermind (a new and curious verb I'd learned from civilians), sharing stories and talking about our journeys toward our goals. It was at that conference that I met Jim Hughes and we hit it off (you're going to love his epilogue at the end of this book ... just keep reading!). I also met a chap named Brandon Turner. Brandon had succeeded in real estate and wrote books about it. One of his books is titled *How to (Finally) Write a Wicked-Awesome Book in 100 Days or Less*. Suffice it to say, I was intrigued. I was in a small group with Brandon and found him to be a machine. He spoke a mile a minute but oozed confidence and bravery. Brandon would let nothing stand in his way. He described obstacles he was able to overcome and how he was able to achieve success in business and in writing. Watching him talk, I thought to myself, *"Wait a minute, I've served in the heart of darkness in Afghanistan surrounded by people who wanted to kill me! I can write a book! How scary could it possibly be?"* And so, the seed was planted.

I reconnected with Brandon a few weeks after the conference, picked his brain a bit more, then set about writing my first book, *It's Personal, Not Personnel: Leadership Lessons for the Battlefield and the Boardroom.* I was (and still am) passionate about leadership, loved writing and wanted to fulfill my core purpose in my next journey; writing a leadership book was a perfect fit. My experiences in uniform had hardened me to withstand hardships. I was also stubborn. My stubbornness — which got me in trouble many times in my life — would sure come in handy for this new mission. I did some research on writing, took Brandon's advice, then started. I created an outline first to see if I had something I thought would be useful, something I believed people would buy. Then I got to writing in earnest. On the 2nd of February, 2017, I typed my first words of the book's manuscript. I finished in late May. I never had 100 days as my goal but ended up with a draft manuscript in about 120 days. I'd been out of the Army for less than a year and had accomplished something I was truly proud of.

Authoring a book was a rollercoaster ride. (And it turns out that it always is.) There were days when I was on top, cranking out paragraphs, pages and entire chapters at the speed of light. Then there were other days when I couldn't string a sentence together to save my life. I invested a lot of time in my outline, as coached to do, then, in classic Campbell style, I proceeded to ignore it when writing the book. It probably cost me extra time and frustration but it wouldn't be the first time I blazed a path in ignorance, using brute

Celebrating the publishing of It's Personal, Not Personnel *while visiting with family.*

force and hoping it would all turn out OK. There were entire chapters that needed reconstruction but, in the end it, all came together. I'm proud of that first book, and thrilled to be here finished with my second book, written with *you* in mind.

A PORTFOLIO CAREER

While writing about people-centered leadership for my first book, it occurred to me that I could consult, coach and speak about this topic. It could turn out to be a good income and would certainly be fulfilling. So I took the leap and became a businessman. I established a limited-liability corporation in the spring of 2017, calling it Investing in People Consulting and Coaching, and I started networking to drum up some business. The beginning was very slow. In fact, I would not gain my first paying client until January of 2018. I did a lot of pro bono leadership consulting work and spoke about leadership at several organizations for free, just to get my name out there and gain some credentials. I almost threw in the towel a few times but, thanks to my pension, the USS Campbell didn't sink.

My how times were tight, though. Did I mention that I almost threw in the towel? My first paid client engagement involved a six-month consulting retainer, which was enough to keep the Campbell family balance sheet "balanced." I gave that client my best and then went "on the chase" to gain more clients, all the while keeping a backup plan close at hand, willing to jettison this sinking ship and get a full-time job if it came to that. For a few semesters, I served as an adjunct professor for the U.S. Marine Corps at their satellite Command and Staff College at a local military base; this provided a nice part-time paycheck and was a chance to give back. I've had a handful of paid speaking engagements with large corporations and joined the National Speakers Association (NSA) in an effort to do more paid speaking events.

Bit by bit, it became clear that what I was looking for (and creating) was not a "job" but a path to a portfolio career — where I could invest my talents in multiple areas, like speaking, consulting, teaching and authorship ... all focused on leadership and bringing out the best in others. Without realizing it, I was actually building a *brand* — the Rob Campbell brand. In the Army, we had ranks and assignments, duty stations and deployments. But in the "real world," I needed to establish a reputation ... I needed to be "that leadership consultant who ..."

With this in mind, I became more deliberate about sharing my points of view with various audiences who would listen. Coupled with income-focused activities, I have found fulfillment in lead-generation and brand-building activities, like creating my blog on my website and writing for a military magazine. I've volunteered to serve as an advisory board member for the Military Spouse (MILSPO) Project and as the Vice President for the Association of the United States Army, University of North Carolina, Wilmington Chapter. As I write, I now have had eight paying clients and am seeing more demand for my services. I've been able to meet several business leaders in Wilmington, NC, and am now recognized more (at coffee shops and at business mixers) as I conduct business and participate in other related events locally.

In November of 2018, I was selected One of *Wilmington Business Journal*'s Most Intriguing People of 2018. This gave me the opportunity to speak to more than 400 business owners about the benefits of hiring veterans, another area I am spending more time on. This speech opened some doors for me. I've spoken around town and struck up a few friendships in the process. One connection led to my accepting a part-time leadership role as the executive director of a veteran entrepreneurship program called VetToCEO, an opportunity which excites and inspires me daily. I am definitely not on easy street. Times are still very tight ... with one son still in college and a wife starting her own business.

And, as life would have it, another big change was about to come our way. It turned out that, because we were used to getting a new set of PCS orders every two to three years from the Army, we'd become accustomed to moving around. It turns out, we like it … crave it, even! Military institutionalism at work. So it was time to pack it up and head on to another adventure, leaving the beach behind and trying something new! And we did it in grand fashion. More on that later, I promise.

LOOKING BACK ...

If forced to write an after-action review of the three-year period between my Army retirement and now, it would surely highlight a few key lessons, in no particular order:

1. **I'm thankful that I didn't throw in the towel.** At a few different points, I could have given up on finding the right groove and taking "a job" instead. In fact, I nearly did, and I would have tossed away everything I worked for. I would have turned my back on my passions. I'm glad I persisted and that Leslie had faith and patience too. This said, there are no guarantees in life. While on Topsail Island, I lived close enough to a large military base with lots of contract work and government jobs I'm competitive for. I was also not far from Wilmington, NC, a good-sized city with a large medical center and university. If the bottom fell out, I had options, and options are essential in this unpredictable world. I recognize that everyone reading this book is wired like me or in a similar life stage or situation. Many senior servicemembers retire with younger children and financial demands that cannot withstand the financial unpredictability of entrepreneurship. I could have taken a job out of

the gate and used it as a vehicle to fund my passion-aligned life, and that would have been alright. In fact, it may have been a smoother take-off than chopping my way through the jungle.

If the bottom fell out, I had options, and options are essential in this unpredictable world

2. **The military/civilian transition is hard work and it will not come overnight.** I guess I never thought it would take me two years to achieve a handful of clients. It took every bit of those two years, but if you believe in what you do, approach it smartly, seek advice (like I do with Jim Hughes) and network heavily, success can be yours.

3. **Less is more, and downsizing is all the rage.** That's right, we sold the beach house on Topsail Island, jettisoned a bunch of our stuff and moved to the city. More on that later, but the lesson here is be careful not to drop any big anchors. The house, which we loved and really don't regret buying, was a big anchor and we could not ignore the weight of it as months passed by. One thing to consider is keeping yourself mobile — meaning be able to pick up and move if needed. You will change as you settle into your new life, and you ought to let the change *take* you to places you ought to be.

You will change as you settle into your new life, and you ought to let the change take you to places you ought to be.

4. **Taking time off to breathe, think and plot the next move was smart.** I did most of this recalibrating during my terminal leave period, when I was still receiving my active duty pay. I was not completely comfortable in that space but, in the end, it led to some smarter decisions. I would most definitely elect to do that again. I filled the time with tasks around the house, reading and writing, which helped. I can't watch television or surf the internet all day, though there's nothing wrong with doing so as a respite for a while if that helps you recharge your batteries. Landscaping and lawn work, for me, is therapy. I can process quite a bit and solve many a problem while operating a rake.

5. **Book writing was great but, as yet, has not been a money maker.** I never expected book sales to pay my bills. My first book served as a large business card for me and it continues to do so. I didn't realize until after reading *Big Magic* by Elizabeth Gilbert that when I wrote *It's Personal, Not Personnel*, I wrote the book for myself. Sure, I wanted to help leaders. I still do but the journey of book writing and publishing was one of fulfillment, one of expressing my creativity and even one of healing. I reflect often on my leadership and that first book helped me process my successes and failures in a new way. This book, *At Ease*, has done the same from a health and welfare standpoint. For me, it has been a more formal way of journaling which is a very healthy way to process feelings and worries. And I do know there are many thousands of men and women separating from the military who could use a "friend" through this disorienting journey, so I hope this book will change lives and touch hearts. The royalties are an extra perk (and a fun one too).

6. **I needed to temper my ego when looking for jobs.** While I did very little formal "job hunting," I know that I probably pissed off a few people involved in hiring. I would argue that my lack of certifications like SHRM-CP, CSM (no, not command sergeant major), or CBPA were mitigated by decades of experience leading and problem solving. I'd state with confidence that I could serve as a CEO. Heck, many general officers transitioned from the service into CEO jobs, knowing very little about the products or services offered by their new companies. What mattered most was the large organizational leadership they brought, not their expertise with its product line. Yeah, not many people wanted to hear this. I should not have expected to walk through the door straight to the C-Suite. Live and learn.

7. **LinkedIn is the bee's knees!** For my business, LinkedIn is my community. It is a very professional forum of people in all industries and fields. On there, I can post highlights from my writing and speaking. I've made short videos, shared photos and written articles. My network is nearing 19,000. I'm connected to various communities related to my leadership consulting, such as HR, veterans, CEOs and other leadership consultants and speakers. I'm there daily and give partial credit to LinkedIn for my business success. Anyone transitioning from the service, especially as a senior servicemember, should get on LinkedIn and start building a network now.

PART TWO
PERSPECTIVES AND PHILOSOPHIES

In the early days of the transition, Leslie and I addressed a series of key questions and formed a set of standard operating procedures (SOPs) to guide us — guide being the operative word because we were committed to being flexible and we didn't want to cement ourselves in fixed positions. If conditions changed or our thinking evolved, we would alter our plan. An open mind was required. There was no telling what might lie ahead and we didn't want to enter this open space being stubborn or ignorant. For example ... early on, we decided we would cast a wide net in the job market, taking us practically anywhere, yet we felt an intense loyalty to geography and moved to the North Carolina coast. As time went on, we got more clarity about our philosophies and more grateful for the fresh perspectives that this transition afforded us.

Part 1 of this book was, I'll admit it, very much about me — about this one soldier's story, and what he did, felt and experienced. Now, it's time to jump into Part 2, which is really about you. In this section of the book, I'll do my best to provide you some body armor or fill your magazine with philosophies you can use like bullets for each target that presents itself. Three years after starting our military/civilian transition, my wife and I still use these philosophies and form new ones to manage each milestone, obstacle and decision facing us. That's why I think they may be helpful to you, too. The Army was easy and predictable to an extent, compared to the new path we embarked upon. Regardless of whether you've served in the Army, Navy, Air Force, Marines or Coast Guard, I'm guessing you can relate to that desire (or need!) for structure, timelines and guideposts. So I'm hopeful that providing you a handful of philosophies and guiding principles for the transition might feel comfortable to you, too. Institutionalization runs deep, and a little bit of a field manual is imperative. Think of the perspectives and philosophies in the following pages as information, suggestions, permission or even fuel to drive your decision toward a desired destination.

Chapter 8
CELEBRATE YOUR SERVICE

Bottom line up front: You've dedicated your life to this most honorable and noble profession, the profession of arms. You've served your nation in a time of war. You volunteered to step forward when others did not. You didn't do it alone. Your family or some other person or persons stood by your side. You should *celebrate* your career and service.

While all this may seem a bit cliché and over mentioned, it is worth noting and deserving of the paragraphs ahead. Looking back, I am glad I celebrated my service in a formal and joyful way. I've known too many servicemembers who didn't. Some just slipped out the back door quietly and rode off into the sunset. Some attended the mandatory group retirement ceremony, which many services conduct, shed their uniform and then turned their back. I don't bring this up as a criticism of those who slip away quietly. In fact, I understand why they do. This lack of pause, reflection and celebration happens for a variety of reasons. Maybe a bad boss or bad experience in the latter part of your career has caused you to be bitter or depleted and eager to walk away. Or maybe you have big plans for what's next, and you're so focused on the next job, house or life that you're inclined to sprint in that direction the moment you are free. Or you might just want to skip the fanfare or not inconvenience people with a ceremony. Whatever your reasoning and whatever your plan, take this part of the book into consideration.

What's with this celebration stuff anyway? Why do it? What purpose can it possibly serve? After all, you know what you've done. And your family is likely a bit worn by all the pomp and circumstance prevalent in the military. How about you take the family or your support network out for burgers and beer, wearing jeans and ball caps and call it a career? What's all the fuss about?

Burgers and beer, I confess, are always fun. But would it be enough to celebrate the life chapter you are about to close? Perhaps a more formal celebration of your success is in order. Julian Illman and Kathryn Bryant of *Brilliant Living HQ* wrote an article that is (ironically enough) pretty brilliant when it comes to this very topic, and they called it "6 Reasons Why We Should Celebrate Success."[1] This article is a perfect fit for a transitioning senior servicemember, with five out of six of their "reasons" hitting home for us military types.

- **Number 2 on the list: Development of a Success Mindset.** As military leaders, most of us won't retire at the age of 75 and pick up a fishing pole. We have plenty of fuel in our tanks and more achievements ahead of us. Celebrating your success is a perfect ingredient for the development of your success mindset as you head out on what may be a very foreign experience. You'll need a success mindset in the jungle of the big world.

- **Reasons to Celebrate, Numbers 3, 4 and 5: Motivation, Feeling Good and Happy Chemicals.** I am sure you can recall several key achievements throughout your career. Remember how they felt and how they motivated you to perform even better? Drag

---

1   https://www.brilliantlivinghq.com/6-reasons-why-you-should-celebrate-success/

all those moments back up, look at your career holistically and recognize the success and growth of your family as one big, badass achievement. Speak about it, tell the world as you depart the military. The Happy Chemical or dopamine released in our brains when we achieve success causes us to want more of it, according to Illman and Bryant. Stepping out of uniform into the next challenge with a nice dose of dopamine is what the body needs.

- **Number 6: Sharing Success.** This one is often overlooked, in my experience. Consider a younger servicemember or professional in attendance at your retirement celebration. Sharing your story and successes might be the motivation they need to succeed like you have. You've just finished a career, setting the example for younger servicemembers to emulate your successes. Give the people in your audience another dose of that. Celebrate your success.

We did it! You and I. We served in a time of war and most cannot fathom that. We served a cause and gave of ourselves selflessly. We touched thousands of lives. We made a difference. I realize I am headed down the cliché road, but I hope you'll pause for a moment and consider the journey. Look at your family and recall the family that existed (if it did) when you began your career. Think about the gates you needed to pass through to achieve the rank and position you did. I remember a moment of pride at Fort Benning, Georgia, in the latter part of my career. I was an Army Ranger, Paratrooper, Jumpmaster and had been through all the testing, pain and suffering the Army's Infantry School could dole out. I felt proud and nostalgic being on an installation that used to intimidate the hell out of me. I commanded paratroopers and soldiers in combat. I made a difference in the lives of servicemembers and family members. My family and I survived and thrived through three deployments, long separations, housing inspectors, busted furniture, hard bosses, and schools that failed to cater to our children. Our sons were born in military hospitals and raised as "Army brats." We were and still are an Army family. Just thinking about the scale of what we have overcome and experienced as a family stirs up my emotions. Many of the civilians I encounter in this post-military life marvel over what I and my family endured and enjoyed. It is no small affair.

· ·

We were and still are an Army family. Just thinking about the scale of what we have overcome and experienced as a family stirs up my emotions.

· ·

SHARE THE PRIDE

It's not about you. Yes, after all that praise, I'm going to remind you that, when it comes to celebrating your service, it's not really about you. This is not to marginalize your service, but think of it this way: the family — who stood by you for years and helped you achieve the rank and years of service you did — are deserving of

The Campbell family's final farewell to the Army. Rob's retirement ceremony (Washington, DC, 2016).

recognition too. Most of you who are reading this book have experienced countless recognition ceremonies or farewells, where you were placed in the spotlight and hailed for your accomplishments. Now is your time to place your family on center stage. At the end of your career, you are probably decorated with medals and qualification badges reflective of a career of service. They are not. This career was yours, not theirs. Your spouse, whose needs are often second to the needs of the military, may have been held from a career and desires of his or her own. Your children were probably pulled from schools and friends they loved. They likely suffered during your absences and celebrated their own achievements without you present. This was the case in my own family and, for that reason, I wanted to express my admiration of them in front of others. Along with this recognition, I wanted to express how grateful we were to have grown our family in a values-based society. We were grateful for the opportunity to live in some great locations and grow together. It was time to place the spotlight of gratitude on my wife and sons, and to thank the Army too.

When I handed over command of the 1st Brigade, 101st Airborne Division to my successor in what would end up being a year before my retirement, the Army conducted a large traditional parade and ceremony to celebrate my command tour, to commemorate the accomplishments of my soldiers and to recognize my wife and family. That, being the hallmark of my career, could have served as my final farewell. As I handed off the brigade flag, I had not yet decided on retirement but I did understand the value of celebration and gratitude. I assembled many of the same people I'd assemble later, at my retirement, and I had an opportunity to express my thanks. But celebrating a change in command is not quite the same thing as celebrating an entire career.

After thinking it over and speaking with friends, I determined that there needed to be one final event. This would celebrate 27 years of service — far beyond my brigade command — and would include as many people as I could muster, ones who were with me and made a difference in my life and career from the very start. I was at NORTHCOM for the final year of my career, and was sure to receive an award for my time there (along with a small ceremony), but it would be insufficient to recognize a 27-year journey. Moreover, few people in that vast headquarters knew who I was or had been with me in my Army years. I could have asked to be included in the monthly retirement ceremony at Fort Carson (the nearest Army base). Or I could have elected to just "slip away," in airborne jargon, on to a distant drop zone never to be seen again. But I knew this moment needed to be marked in a special way, not for me, but for everyone around me. I would host a ceremony, celebrate my service, thank and showcase my family, and close out a very proud and defining chapter in my life. I'm so glad I did.

We decided that Washington, DC, would be a great place to host a ceremony. My official retirement date was October 31, 2016, so we thought anytime in October would be great. I asked a mentor and friend of mine, Major General Andrew P. Poppas, to host the ceremony and conduct my retirement. I would invite family, military friends and even my old college roommate, who was there at the beginning, when I enlisted in the Army National Guard as a college freshman. I asked some of my beloved staff members from the 101st Airborne to narrate and provide the invocation to the event. I had been to enough ceremonies and knew enough about protocol that I could create a simple yet appropriate script. The best part was that it was my event and would be conducted my way, loosely but appropriately following military protocol.

I needed something to present to my family members. I had seen another senior servicemember buy and present family member medals she purchased at MilitaryWives.com. I bought and framed child medals and a spouse medal to present to my family. As for me, I was awarded the Defense Superior Service Medal for my time at NORTHCOM and I would use that medal again in this ceremony. I had my Army retirement pin and folded American flag, which were handed to me in an unceremonious way by a civilian staff member in the transition office at Fort Carson. I would have all of these presented by MG Poppas as a recognition of service. We conducted the ceremony on Fort Myer, Virginia, which was a good central location for all our East Coast family to gather, and it happened to be where MG Poppas lived. I rented a spot in the officer's club and helped arrange some room reservations on the base. I had done plenty of formal event planning in my career, so this was very familiar. The Campbells would go out with a bang. It turned out to be a memorable event. MG Poppas was eloquent as always, and paid a fitting tribute not only to my service but to my family's service as well. We were able to reunite with people we had not seen in years but who had a positive influence on our lives. It was wonderful celebration and memory we will treasure for the rest of our lives.

I needed to deliver one of the most important speeches of my career and life. I dedicated months thinking about what I would say and weeks preparing fitting remarks. It would be my last big moment in uniform. Reflecting, as I had done in abundance since the day my retirement was approved, I had strong feelings of gratitude and wonder for all we had experienced. I suspected there might be many who wondered what happened — why I chose to leave a remarkable career. I was

Rob with warrior brothers at his retirement ceremony (Washington, DC, 2016).

in a relatively small society as an infantry Colonel, and I wanted to quell any rumors that might crop up about my departure. I felt guilt about those who I would leave behind, those who were counting on me to make a difference in our Army (and a difference in their own lives and careers). I felt that I might be disappointing many leaders and mentors who had invested in me — those who may have hoped I would rise to the rank of general and continue to serve. I wanted to communicate all they had given to me, and reflect on the lessons that I planned on carrying forward into my next life. I wanted to assure them that their investment in me was not in vain. Mostly, I wanted to thank the assembled crowd, my family and the Army.

Below is an excerpt of this speech, which captures my feelings and gratitude. It may help you reflect on your own career, its meaning and impact on you and your family.

. . . .

A GRATEFUL SOLDIER
October 2016

Thank you. You will hear that a lot this speech. We are so grateful that all of you are here. "Overwhelmed" is probably a better way to put it. Well, here goes … my last speech in uniform. First to Major General Poppas. I asked him to host this event and now everyone knows why. Sir, you have done so — as you always do — with a very personal touch. This is a day I will never forget. MG Poppas is an officer who doesn't take himself and his job too seriously, but rather enjoys life, those he is surrounded by and sets command climates that people flock to. Sir, you're a hell of a soldier and I'm proud to have served with you and, more importantly, to call you a friend. I am part of long list of warriors who get to say with pride, "Yeah, I served with Poppas."

The title of this speech is "A Grateful Soldier." That's what I am today. So unbelievably grateful for what the Army has given my family and me. First, let's squash any rumors. I haven't hit a brick wall, lost faith or received a bad report. It's just time for the Campbells, for many reasons. I don't expect all to understand. It's OK. Retirement is a personal decision, after all … one that needs to fit for us. I've been making some very important decisions for 27 years. Trust that I have this one right.

I have to say that the hardest part of choosing to retire was the fact that many people were counting on me and had hoped that I would stay in, get promoted, help lead the Army into its ambiguous future, serve with them again. I'm touched by that. I do want everyone to know, especially all of you gathered here, that your investment in me, superior and subordinate, was not in vain. I will find a way to continue to do what I was put on this earth to do — to make a difference in the lives of others through optimistic leadership. It just won't happen in uniform. I think the world could use a dose of optimistic leadership.

So, there I was, a college freshman, 175 pounds, hair parted in the middle. 1986. I still remember the signs posted all over the dorm freshman year. "Join the Massachusetts Army National Guard" — free tuition, $2,000 sign-up bonus, weekend drill pay. Translated: beer money! That's right ... it wasn't about a sense of patriotism or call to duty. So it started for Private Campbell ... infantry basic training, Fort Benning, Georgia, shaven head, living in old World War II barracks with the big industrial fans in the Georgia summer heat, wearing a steel pot helmet and old woodland battle-dress uniform with black leather boots. It seems like ages ago.

The Army has done so much for me. The Rob Campbell who first donned this uniform in the late 1980s was, I confess, a bit selfish, spoiled and frankly not quite as ethical as I needed to be. Uncle Sam quickly went to work on those demons and baptized me an officer. Spring 1989, my father-in-law, a Vietnam veteran, commissions me a second lieutenant in the infantry. My dad, a reservist, received the silver dollar for my first salute, a tradition. Back in the day, I wasn't the sharpest knife in the drawer. Perhaps that hasn't changed much! I graduated with a 2.6 GPA, fighting my way into an Army that didn't really need many lieutenants. Almost immediately, I found myself surrounded by officers of great intellect, physical fitness — leaders I could emulate, like many in this room. I had to work extra hard to catch up, but I did, even bypassing some of them along the way.

It was only in my latter years in uniform, looking back, that I realized how grateful I was to have lived in this environment of values and ethics and selfless service, surrounded by soldiers and scholars, men and women, of all races and from all corners of our nation and the world. I'm grateful not only for what it has done to me but as I have watched my two sons mature, I can see the influence living in a values-based society has had on them — two fine young men I remain enormously proud of. Leslie and I have grown and expanded our horizons in so many ways, thrust into new environments and hardened by combat. So, as the Campbell family steps out into the world, we do so better prepared, and we have the Army to thank for it.

27 years, 5 months, 7 days. This journey has been a wild roller coaster ride of ups and downs … mostly ups. Incredible places and people that have enriched us in so many ways. Command Sergeant Major Johnny Austin, First Corps, Fort Lewis, put it very well when he retired. He said, "The Army was the opportunity of a lifetime for a lifetime of opportunity." We had the opportunity to serve in some fantastic places, like Fort Lewis, Washington, where we got to hang with my sister Melissa and watch her family grow and where we got to experience the Pacific Northwest. Hawaii, where we joined the Golden Dragon Battalion of the 25th Infantry Division, Tropic Lightning, represented by several of my brothers in the audience. (Good to see you and your lovely ladies, men. I'm giving you all a three-day pass.) Five years in the 82nd Airborne Division as a major which sucked the life out of me! No kidding. (There is a pump at the gate at Fort Bragg.) I'm enormously grateful for my time in a parachute harness with the All Americans, especially the Panther Brigade. Alaska, which came out of left field. I tried to fight it until Leslie told me to shut my mouth and follow orders. No kidding. It turned out to be absolutely fantastic commanding 1-40 Cavalry Airborne. I'd go back to Alaska

*in a heartbeat. (In summer.) Germany. Wow, that didn't suck! What
an experience! Then Fort Campbell and the 101st Screaming Eagles.
I always wanted to serve in the 101st and hit the lottery getting selected
to command 1st Brigade, the Bastogne Brigade, and stand on the
shoulders of numerous leaders who went before me.*

*Three combat tours, one in Iraq and two to Afghanistan, where
I fought alongside the most courageous and selfless men and women
I have ever met. In those faraway places, I was immersed among
a population of incredibly poor people in the harshest of environments. It left a lasting impact on me. Like many of you, I lost friends
and soldiers, and though I take off the uniform for the last time, they
will forever live in my heart.*

*My gratitude today goes to many of you in this audience and countless
others who took a chance on me, underwrote my mistakes, showed
me a better way. I embark on this next chapter with you as the proverbial angel on my shoulder. So if I am about do to something selfish,
be lazy or even drift toward the dark side of unethical behavior, there
you will be — a shout from Drill Sergeant Robertson to pick my head
up off the ground, or Captain Brettmann to add a dose of common
sense to the plan, a fatherly gaze from General Hill as if to say "Rob,
just because you can do that it doesn't mean you should" or Major
General Howard, "Rob, picture a long sub sandwich and one packet
of mustard. You spread the mustard over the long sub roll and soon
you can't taste it. Don't spread yourself too thin, you'll accomplish
nothing." Or a course adjustment from one of my trusty majors.
"Sir, slow down and let's develop a plan before you push the launch
button." I'm grateful. You'll always be with me.*

*To my wife Leslie. Retired General Jay Garner said it very well. If he
had two decisions in his life to make again, he would marry the same
woman and join the United States Army. Nicely put. My, we have come
a long way. 16 moves in 27 years, numerous exercises away from home,*

two last-minute c-sections, two wonderful sons, five cats (I think), two dogs, three combat deployments, and the list goes on. I've been lying to her for years. "Rob, when are you coming home?" "Very soon, not much on the plate this afternoon, honey." Yeah, right. I love her to the moon. There is no Colonel Rob Campbell without Leslie. She keeps me grounded and in check.

Let me share a story. So you can imagine the ego boost I get from being the commander of infantry formations training to close-with and destroy the enemy. My giant ego and I squeeze through the door each night and she so gently reminds me of the level of authority I really have. So there we were — Fort Campbell, Kentucky, home of the 101st Airborne Division Air Assault, the Screaming Eagles, the band of brothers. I commanded one of its three infantry brigades. That's code for "I'm the man!" So, I'm fresh from a training event where we conducted a large-scale brigade air assault. Picture, if you will, an endless sea of helicopters chopping the air from the sky with their rotors, soldiers postured on the pick-up zone in full kit ready for combat, artillery pieces slung under heavy-lift helicopters, and I'm in my command-and-control bird — commanding this brigade air assault operation, on the radio giving orders to my commanders, in my element, the brigade combat team commander. Puddles of testosterone all over the floor of the helicopter. The true essence of the 101st. The most mobile combat unit in the history of warfare. So, I sit down to dinner and she very casually says "How was your helicopter ride?"

God bless you, honey. I get all the recognition. I stand up here with a chest full of ribbons and medals, get formally recognized by soldiers and leaders for my accomplishments. Her, less so, but make no mistake — her accomplishments run deep and are profound. Countless Army families she touched, spouses she mentored, volunteer hours for the betterment of every Army community we served in. Raising two amazing dudes, watching me head off to combat and assuming the dual role of mom and dad, living out of suitcases for months at a time, sleeping on blow-up mattresses, the list goes on. I have navigated this career embracing each assignment, my duties, and all that came with it, but that's me. She didn't sign up for this. Some days, I was reminded of that. But, man, did she deliver ... no matter what I or the Army asked of her. With poise, grace and a dump truck load of love, she thrust herself out of bed in the middle of the night to meet returning soldiers, delivered healing remarks to a battalion's worth of grieving families at the memorial ceremonies for fallen soldiers, and was a source of light and support at countless other events.

She is my better half. She's my introvert and I'm her extrovert. She's the flower child and I'm the field marshal. She lets me hold the remote control, gives me the big piece of chicken, she makes me feel like a man. She won't admit it but it must have hurt when she fell down from heaven. She's a national treasure and I'm sure glad I didn't have to do this Army stuff without her. Would you please stand and help me recognize a superb example of an Army wife? My wife Leslie.

To the Campbell pipe-swinger wrecking machines, Robbie and Louden. Boys, your mom and I are so very proud of you both. Robbie is a film design rock star, building a life for himself in Utah. Check out his VLOG to see what I mean. Louden has started his freshman year of college. He can play the guitar like a man possessed. Boys, I know this Army life has not always matched your schedule or desires, but I thank you for your perseverance, resilience and for the fine young men you are. You are both going to do amazing things and Mom and I will be cheering from the sidelines. I love you both with all my heart.

So, we have settled on the beach in North Carolina. You are all invited. Not all at once, please. There will be plenty of beach chairs, umbrellas, sunblock lotion and beer. Bring it on. We are 244 steps from the Atlantic Ocean. We are looking forward to beginning the next chapter and hope that all of you will be a part of it in some way. Please stick around and have a beer, and let us say thanks up close. 27 years,

5 months, 7 days. I'd do it all over again. Every minute. To all of you, to the Army, I offer my deepest love respect and gratitude. Army Strong!

. . . .

Chapter 9
HONOR YOUR SPOUSE

....

I'm passionate about a lot of things, not the least of which is the military spouse.

....

This chapter might just be my favorite. I'm passionate about a lot of things, not the least of which is the military spouse. I'm enormously lucky to be married to one of the best. I suspect you gathered that from my retirement speech. I was

Rob and Leslie (Fort Bragg, NC, 2007).

drowning in tears when I wrote that and read it. Hell, I might break down writing this chapter. If you see some text that is blurred, you'll know why. I included this chapter because I believe it is of enormous importance. To consider and experience transition from the military without your spouse or partner is to half step it. I'm sure the military spouse experience was similar for you and yours, but I want to briefly highlight my wife Leslie's journey to illustrate the prominence of the military spouse in this transition to something authentic. Leslie was my girl when I raised my right hand and attended basic training as an infantry private in 1987, and all through my training and accession as an officer. She and my dad pinned on my gold lieutenant bars in 1989 after her dad swore me in. We made it official when we exchanged wedding vows and, wasting no time and in true Army fashion, I shaved my head and entered Army Ranger School five days later. Some honeymoon! From day one, the Army was a family affair.

Thankfully, Leslie came from good stock. Her mom was a seasoned military spouse. Her dad served in Vietnam as a helicopter pilot and they lived a typical military life seeing him off to combat tours, moving from post to post, and raising

Visiting with family before returning to war. Four generations of warriors: WWII, Korea, Vietnam, Iraq and Afghanistan (Washington, DC, 2010).

children for 10 years active followed by 21 years in the reserves. Of course, her mom served under the "if the Army wanted you to have a family, they would have issued you one" era. I respect her greatly for enduring that. Thankfully, those days are far behind us. Leslie was never subjugated or ignored, like her mom was, and family inclusion was an important part of the military experience for my generation. While soldiers from my era were given the option to "include" their spouses and children in the military experience, the Army previously didn't really hold people accountable in this area. This changed for the better when the Army embraced the concept of "Family Readiness." Readiness meant something. No one questioned combat readiness. We strove for that each day — from PT to night live-fire training. Readying our families became a measurable task for a commander, on par with mission essential task lists (METLs).

Of course, 9/11 and our subsequent wars would take family readiness to where we are today with family wellness programs, steering meetings, plus meaningful training and events to ready the family for the difficulty of combat separation. Leslie witnessed and benefited from the addition of family life counselors and family readiness support assistants, as well as raised awareness and programs to assist families in overcoming the challenges of moving from one state to another. Leslie experienced the full spectrum of what military spouses experience — frequent moves, the struggle to get our children the attention they needed in the countless schools we entered and departed, dealing with last-minute orders taking our family to a completely new and unknown area, and dealing with a military bureaucracy, which often resulted in cumbersome paperwork drills and substandard service on the Army forts we called home. The same theory applied. When the Army sucked, there was nothing worse; when it was great, there was nothing better. Fortunately, the highs beat the lows.

· ·

When the Army sucked, there was nothing worse; when it was great, there was nothing better. Fortunately, the highs beat the lows.

· ·

Ah, the good stuff. Vagabonds from the start, Leslie and I embraced each move and reaped the benefits from living in and exploring garden spots like Hawaii, Germany, Alaska and countless other places the Army sent us. We cherished our family time traversing the country numerous times or trekking across Europe, Alaska and the Hawaiian Islands. We landed some pretty sweet homes, compliments of the military. We were even able to buy a house with an inground pool! Our children, Army brats, were raised in a values-based society.

They gained coping skills and resilience thrust into new environments. They formed life-long friendships and confidence to venture out on their own. All of this was important to Leslie and she remains grateful to the Army. So do I.

. . . .

While Leslie and I remain tremendously proud and nostalgic of our service in a time of war, my combat years were unquestionably the most difficult times.

. . . .

Of course, most of my time in uniform was dominated by combat — the build-up to the deployment, the deployment itself, then the reintegration once home. While Leslie and I remain tremendously proud and nostalgic of our service in a time of war, my combat years were unquestionably the most difficult times. They were difficult in numerous ways.

- *Difficult on our children.* I still do not know how scarred my sons are from this experience. They seem healthy. I know my oldest has nightmares that he and I are waiting in line to use the bathroom and I enter but to not return.

- *Difficult on our marriage.* Being apart and under fire for a year or more is not healthy for a relationship. Leaving Leslie to care for two terrified boys was not something we discussed before deciding to marry. The constant cloud that hung over us as we approached another deployment was the ever-present elephant in the room in every moment of our lives. It still conjures up anxiety and that nervous pit you feel in your stomach when you know hardship is ahead.

- *Difficult during reintegration.* I confess I screwed it up the first time, reinserting myself into a family that had grown accustomed to living without me.

- *Difficult in the conversations we had about how to handle the loss or serious injury of a soldier.* Leslie was by my side and often out in front through this. As my "First Lady," she led and cared for the families of my unit before, during and after our deployments. I'd call Leslie on a satellite phone from Afghanistan when we lost a soldier and she would muster up the courage to deliver healing remarks to the families of our unit traumatized by the news or rally a group of spouses to provide assistance to a family in need. Not to mention, through all of this she endured the difficulty of having her husband in harm's way and a television dominated by the horrifying images of war.

My wife's service (though she did not raise her right hand or draw a paycheck, she *served* nonetheless), could be typified by the words selflessness and sacrifice. It seemed that she always took a back seat — a back seat to my career, a back

The artist, Leslie, blazing her own path.

seat to the needs of me and our children, and a back seat to everyone else's careers. Save for a short stint teaching, Leslie did not work in the formal sense. She was a stay-at-home mom which I considered a full-time job with lots of overtime. Together, we decided that she would stay at home, raise our children and care for our home wherever the military sent us. It was a heavy lift for her, and she did it with grace. She is an artist and, as our sons grew older and more self-sufficient, she expanded her art portfolio and network. However, just as her artist network grew and she began to blossom, the Army would swoop in and whisk us away to another installation, causing her to have to start over. I had a prominent office in all my assignments, surrounded by a supporting staff. She occupied the spare bedroom or basement to set up her art studio in each of the places we served. She did a lot and I always felt this burning desire to pay her back. I still do. And she still sacrifices. I guess it is in her DNA.

YOUR SPOUSE'S TIME TO SHINE

Those who have served in the past few decades probably have a similar story about their spouse. Perhaps it is time to place them in the spotlight and give them the priority. When Leslie and I began our discussions about separation, her desires received the same focus as mine. Throughout our marriage, she would be the last one to put her foot down and demand something or issue an ultimatum, so going into the transition, she didn't create a list of wants ... but I desired to focus more on her than I had previously. I wanted her to have something inspiring and wonderful in this next life, unspoiled by a set of orders or a combat deployment. Soon, we would be empty-nesters and deep into this next journey, and no longer did I want her art studio in the basement or spare bedroom. We would not be instantly wealthy, but I didn't want her to sacrifice anymore. I didn't want her in the back seat any longer. Once transitioned, I could accomplish this with far less risk. Fortunately, we desired a lot of the same things, like the freedom to travel, the ability to see and care for our parents, and the mystery of the next assignment or combat deployment gone. We wanted greater control of our lives and a chance to watch our kids take to the world with less distraction.

Here is how it all went down ...

Of course, this story would begin by Leslie taking one more for the team. As I've shared in previous chapters, we decided that Leslie should take a job to help us with the transition. She knew it was a big step for me and all of us, so she wanted to do her part as always. Approaching the abyss and facing a cut in pay, we did not truly understand what our finances would look like. But having bought a house and needing to educate our youngest child through college, we knew the financial demands would be there. That temporary job lasted a year, and back to her art studio she went. This time she would not be in the basement, but would reign over a huge room on the bottom floor of our beach house. The previous owner used that room as a man cave but it was tailor-made to be an artist's studio. It was an open space with a utility closet, bathroom, sufficient lighting, its own porch facing the Atlantic Intracoastal Waterway, and climate control. *She had arrived!* With ample space, she could finally spread out and focus on her craft in comfort.

In no time flat, Leslie opened a business, Ravenworks Studio, which is thriving today (learn more about her art in the Keep in Touch section of the book!). In addition to settling into new rhythms and roles, we

Leslie with her art on display, selected to appear in the Wilmington Business Journal's annual "Book on Business" (2019).

were able to travel with a new sense of freedom. It was strange and wonderful. I was tinkering in the garage one day, scratching my new beard, when Leslie came in and informed me that our 30th high school reunion was coming up. We had not gone to our reunions over the years because of logistics, the kids and, of course, my demanding schedule. Those days of turning down big invitations were gone, and she suggested we go. I was initially resistant; the grips of the military still hanging on and old habits dying hard, as it were. But I quickly saw the light. Moreover, she wanted to do this and she was right. It would be a trip to see our old high school buddies after 30 years. With no approval needed, no young children to care for or schedules to synchronize, off we went. It was liberating and we had an absolute

blast. In fact, it allowed us
to reconnect to some dear
friends we had not seen in
three decades — friends we
are still close with today.
Nice call, Les!

Fall and winter came on
quickly, and we thoroughly
enjoyed the holidays with
family and friends — holidays which had been taken
from us in our previous
life. Louden completed his

*Rob and Leslie take a post-retirement
cross-country trip to see Robbie and
Meggie in Utah.*

freshman year of college, was accepted to transfer to the University
of North Carolina Asheville and he took a summer job on the island.
Later that summer, we dropped him off hours west of home. Without
a job to rush back to, Leslie and I decided to keep heading west to
visit our oldest son, Robbie, and his future wife Meggie in Utah. We
got Louden all set up in his dorm, registered for classes and situation
for college life, then said a tearful goodbye. Our last one was off to
college. We did it. We could barely compose ourselves as he disap-
peared from our sight to join his classmates.

Art supplies, check. Easel, check. Change of socks, check. We were
loaded and ready to head west. It was a unique and free-form kind
of vacation, and we were giddy. On the schedule, visits with family,
beautiful scenery and Airbnb adventures. It was wonderful in so
many ways. Our children were engaged in their busy lives and we
were off on an adventure, not worried about them. Once this truly
special trip was in the history books, we found ourselves back on
the island, reunited with our cats. Leslie started to branch out and
connect with local galleries and form friendships on the island with
neighbors and other artists. It was fun watching her take off.

Before we knew it, it was 2018. One day in the kitchen, in a fit of excitement, Leslie announced that we would be going to France that summer. She had applied for an artist residency and included me as a writer in residence. We were selected. *What?* I was shocked initially and concerned with how we could pull it off financially. Once again, the Army colonel reared his ugly head and wanted to ask all the hard questions about the "operation." I bottled him up. "Tell me more honey!" Once again, she was right. This would be the opportunity of a lifetime and we had complete freedom to do it — freedom we did not previously enjoy before our military/civilian transition. It was amazing and we did it right. Putting some money aside, we included an additional week in Paris. That's right, three weeks in France without a leave form!

We Airbnb'd in a sweet flat in Paris in the month of June and took in the city once again. (we had been to Paris once while in the military, but only for a day). I scraped up enough cash and we rented a car to drive ourselves to our "residency" location — a chateau in the Champagne region of France. It was gorgeous. Leslie set up shop in a palatial room at the end of this historic French chateau. And I created a space to write in our temporary home in the village. I would write all day and break for a nap by the church in the village with the hammock Leslie bought me for my 50th birthday! Leslie blossomed. I never saw her so inspired and at peace. We formed friendships with the other 12 residency attendees and embraced this magical experience.

LOOKING BACK ...

I wish I could take credit for all the wonder Leslie introduced me to in the years following retirement. I will say that I held true to my desire to make her a greater priority in our lives. As usual, she would end up being the one to show me the way. Whatever your plan for transition, consider your spouse in a fresh new light. Take a back seat for once or commit to something together that you always wanted to do but could not because of the demands of your service.

A friend of mine now stays at home and cares for his kids while his wife continues her career. Another friend took some money from the sale of a home and took a year off to spend quality time with his wife and little boy. His Facebook posts were amazing and I know it did wonders for his health and wellbeing. Another friend returned to Italy after his transition, a place his wife fell in love with (so much so that she learned to speak Italian). He has a job there but they are balancing that with a lifestyle, as seen through his many social media posts. I know his wife is in her element. He is too.

> This next journey ought to be different and amazing, not more of the same sacrifice.

You don't have to fly away to France or Airbnb your way across the country, but maybe your spouse wants to return to school or take up a new hobby. Give that some serious thought and, more importantly, make it a priority ... as your career surely was. This next journey ought to be different and amazing, not more of the same sacrifice.

Chapter 10
REDIRECT YOUR VALUES

I lived and continue to live the values of all the services, whether **Commitment** for the Navy and Marine Corps, or **Excellence in All That We Do** for the Air Force. The seven Army Leadership Values — **Loyalty**, **Duty**, **Respect**, **Selfless Service**, **Honor**, **Integrity** and **Personal Courage** (LDRSHIP) — flowed through my veins. Don't get me wrong ... I wasn't this perfect Boy Scout-like guy, who woke up each morning reciting these values like a mantra, or one who walked around and corrected all the non-believers. I'd violate a few of these from time to time, like when I might become selfish about something or not give a person or group the respect they deserved. But the values are part of me. As with all the services, the Army sure did its job. These values were always calling to me, whispering in my ear, keeping me on course. Every training course we took, every inspirational speech we received from military leaders, every historical vignette or battlefield we studied radiated service values. I was a military leader and knew I would be held to these values, so I would talk about them often ... especially when admonishing a servicemember or leader in my organization. This is why it was so difficult to make the decision to retire. As I mentioned in Chapter

5, retiring from the Army was so hard for me because it felt like
a violation of the very code I had vowed to espouse and uphold.

As I entered my post-military life, I knew that I would never abandon
the values of Respect, Honor, Integrity and Personal Courage. Indeed,
I would commit myself to a new cause and my new missions and
always strive for excellence. I would most definitely need these in
the days ahead and still do today, but I needed to reexamine and
reapply Loyalty, Duty, Selfless Service, Commitment and Excellence.
While still in uniform, through my transition, I could still be the
great soldier, leader and person I always strove to be but, through it,
I would need to apply these values differently. I was about to depart
the service for the rest of my life. I would leave the somewhat predictable and safe nest of the military and venture into the woods. This
was a big step in so many ways. In the military, I didn't have to worry
about so many things. I had insurance, a roof over my head and, as
my mother-in-law always said, "the eagle always shits" (meaning
Uncle Sam would always pay me). Save for the assurance of retirement pay, the time to float into the deep end of the pool and either
sink or swim had come.

· ·

Save for the assurance of retirement pay, the time to float into
the deep end of the pool and either sink or swim had come.

· ·

The ways in which I thought about Loyalty and Duty would need to
shift; my new loyalty and duty was to myself and my family, instead
of to the Army. Commitment would be commitment to myself and
the transition process, and not the service. Excellence would shift
from excellence as a soldier to excellence as a transitioning servicemember. Again, I did not turn my back on those I served but my
priorities and my loyalty would need to shift toward me. My duty
would be to a well-executed retirement. I would attend transition

seminars as my place of duty and priority over a work event during my final months in uniform. Whereas before I would cancel medical appointments or miss a family event for a unit event, now the reverse was true. I would hand off some events to my deputy and other teammates. Where I could reschedule events around my work demands, I would ... but I had to take a conscious stand to shift my loyalty over to the transition process. This is why I could not have announced my retirement during my time as a commander. My unit demanded and deserved too much of me. My commitment would always default to those I commanded and their families. The mindset shift (and redirection of my values) could only fully, meaningfully happen during a clean-boots kind of assignment such as I was enjoying at NORTHCOM.

I've got to admit that after a lifetime of "selfless service," learning to practice *selfish* service was incredibly hard. It felt like a daily out-of-body experience to even utter the word "selfish" and place my needs above the institution. Some days, even up to my final days, the Army got all of me but, to get it right, I had to force myself to think and act this new way. I had spent 27 years serving the Army and my soldiers and families; now I had to serve myself. I would need to schedule medical appointments, conduct research and education on the transition, and determine how best to handle what lay ahead and how best to set myself up for success on the outside. The Army would live through my selfishness and, quite frankly, would do little to measure how well I was prepared for the future. Again, I had absolutely no intention of leaving these values in the closet with my uniform. Indeed, I carried them proudly into my next life. "Selfish service" only helped me cater to my needs during a substantial change in my life. To approach it any other way would be a disservice to myself and my family.

MY FINAL SUMMER

NORTHCOM was planning a large training exercise to take place in June 2016, and this big initiative held the attention and priority of everyone in the command. I would show my loyalty to the organization by helping it get through this big exercise, then I would turn completely toward me. Spreading retirement-focused events across the spring and early summer, I would exercise Selfish Service, Loyalty and Duty toward myself yet I would balance, where I could, my duty and commitment to help the organization achieve excellence in the upcoming exercise. I was transparent to my team and my boss about this approach and thankfully all understood. Once the exercise ended in early June, I would hand the reins off to my deputy as if I were on leave and completely focus on the final stage of my transition. There were no absolutes. I always stood ready to jump back in and lead if a crisis were to occur. I had a timeline and, though it could always be adjusted with the proper reasoning and leadership assistance, the clock would continue to tick. So I kept forging ahead. It would be August (the start of my leave) before I knew it, and time for goodbye.

LOOKING BACK ...

Our internal struggles with values and a need to redirect them is likely a universal challenge for transitioning servicemembers, but not something that's easy to articulate. In fact, I never really thought of it as formally as I have just done in these pages, though turning toward myself was a very prevalent feeling and approach before and after my Army retirement. I was glad that I shared this shifting mindset with my team, as they would likely have seen me very differently had I not. Luckily, they understood the gravity of this move and were very supportive.

I did stumble a bit in the early days; mindset shifts are hard. I catered to my unit's needs and pushed aside my own, punting on a few appointments. I always subscribed to the belief that "one person cannot be everything to an organization" or "the strength of a team is how well it performs in the absence of its boss." But when it came to stepping back from the Army to prepare myself to retire, this was easier said than done. Looking back, I realize I should have listened more closely to and subscribed better to this philosophy.

It should be said that, hard as I tried to put myself and Leslie first during this period of our lives, I didn't take an extreme approach. I never became 100% selfish, ignoring the needs of my people and organization. But I needed to *think* of it in extremes and apply it appropriately as I went through the process.

My advice to you is simple but hard: Once you make the call to separate from military service and your separation is approved, consider this reversal-of-values approach and apply it to your milestones or to-do list for transition. You will serve both yourself and your organization well if you can unapologetically embrace the need for reprioritization and new focus.

Chapter 11
CHART YOUR COURSE

Job or geography? It was a question that Leslie and I asked ourselves in several different ways. Even if we were with the people we loved and had a healthy compensation package, would we be happy living in a city that we didn't actively *choose*? No. OK, so much for an open mind! Here's the thing, though ... I would definitely explore that as a possibility, as it would bring some measure of happiness through job fulfillment and, at the end of the day, Leslie and I were close as a couple and would find our happy place somehow. But we hated the cold, for example. Really, really hated the cold. Why would we subject ourselves to a frigid, windy northern city if we didn't have to? Nothing against the great cities of the north. I was born and raised in

Rob and Leslie, enjoying the freedom they fought and sacrificed to protect (Topsail Island, NC, 2017).

Massachusetts, and still have a special place in my heart for Boston. So, who knows? Just watch, you'll connect with me on Facebook or LinkedIn and my profile with have a cold, blustery city as my home. But seriously, there were no beaches (by our North Carolina definition) or mountains up there. And it was cold. Did I mention that?

I never turned down a networking opportunity and I told my coach to cast a wide net for opportunities aligned with my skills and passions, but we could not ignore our aversion to cold-weather geographies and felt especially selfish entering this next phase. Was there no job in a warmer climate that would provide me fulfillment? We certainly believed there *was*. With a pension and a solid resume, you should be able to land at or near where you desire to be.

Job or geography comes down to risk. Are you able to risk being in the place you love, even if it means you might be challenged finding a job or take on a long commute to the nearest city? What would be your contingency plan if the bottom fell out of your encore life and career? Would you head to a remote tropical island in the Pacific? That's probably a stretch on retired pay (though not impossible). The key is risk mitigation. My risk mitigator was being near (though far enough away) from a military base and a decent-sized city where I could find some employment.

Job or geography? The military told you where to live for your entire career. You should consider reversing that. Leslie and I didn't want to wait until we were 70 to finally land in the area we loved. The time was now. We, not the military, would write this PCS order.

HOW TO CHOOSE YOUR NEW ZIP CODE: TIPS FOR CHARTING YOUR OWN COURSE:

There's no perfect strategy for deciding where to go next. But it's *your* call! Use some of that military decision making you are so good at.

List out some decision criteria for you and your family and keep an open, imaginative mind. Here are some ideas to spark your thinking and your conversations:

1. **Consider all the duty stations where you've lived.** What were the pros and cons of living in those areas? For instance, we didn't like the frequent winds and rapidly changing climate of one fort where we were stationed. Another was a bit run down and depressing for our tastes. We loved the diverse landscapes (beaches and mountains) of another posting. One place we lived had the perfect climate but it was so far away from family. Were there any places you lived and served where you can imagine enjoying the next phase of your life?

2. **Look at a map and mark the locations where your loved ones reside** – your parents, siblings, dear friends, adult children. In the next phase of your life, will it be important for you to be nearby these special people?

3. **Be honest about your relationship with Mother Nature.** Are you a ski bunny and a lover of snow? Or have you been waiting all your life to throw away your coats and scarves? Do you feel your happiest in a boat on a lake, or do you dream about hiking through the hills or mountains? Remember, you can go anywhere.

4. **Now consider healthcare as a decision criteria.** We lived on military installations that had their own medical facilities. If they were not on the base, they were not far away and Uncle Sam covered the cost. While living days away from civilization sounds enticing, your remoteness may not be so sexy after all if it means that the ambulance shows up a few hours after you called it.

5. **Work.** You don't have to nail down what industry you wish to work in or even what company but you can position yourself near

a big job market like a large city. You don't even have to decide you want to get a job. Remember that having options is the best way to mitigate risk and gives you the psychological comfort you and your family deserve. I run my own business and don't want to work for anyone but I would and might someday. Because I chose to live where I did and because I worked hard at establishing a network, I have options.

6. **Taxes.** Some states don't tax military retired pay. And some states don't have state income tax either. This can be a factor in your decision. We knew that North Carolina would tax our pay but we desired to live there and still do. Do some math and make the call!

7. **Education.** We were very focused on education while serving, as we moved from base to base. I recall countless conversations with people already living where we would PCS about the schools (K-12 and college), which ones to pick and not pick. Add to this a desire for continuing education that you or your spouse might have. Lastly, consider state residency. We didn't have it for North Carolina when we first arrived so we opted to educate our son Louden in a community college his first year.

8. **Community.** Give this serious consideration. For the most part, we enjoyed social, connected communities in our military lives. We were spoiled by that. While Leslie and I enjoyed our space, we did thrive as a family being part of a larger community, meaning far outside our immediate neighborhood. We loved the beauty and peacefulness of Topsail Island and we loved our immediate neighbors but beyond that, the island lacked cohesion and oneness. The island was thriving in the summers but it lacked a heartbeat in the winter. What is important to you in a community? Take some time and write out a list, then do some probing like you did prior to a move in the military ... to get a sense of community in places you may desire to live.

LOOKING BACK ...

We don't like to look back with regret but Leslie and I are very honest with ourselves about our decisions. That helps us make smarter ones moving forward. We loved our island home and we loved the beach, but we sprinted there ... believing it was permanent. Perhaps we should have rented or done more homework and analysis using the criteria above. We got family, healthcare, work, education and climate right. We got community wrong. While we loved our neighbors, they were 10-20 years ahead of us in their journey. Leslie and I had too much fuel in our tanks and were more vagabond than most in our zip code. Many decisions can be reversed. We backed out of our house and the community and are happier where we currently reside. Be sure that, when charting your course for your encore life, you keep options open for detours and new adventures along the way.

Chapter 12
BE OPEN TO LEARNING

"C-Suite? What was that?" I felt embarrassed to ask at a business networking event, so I ducked into the latrine (or bathroom, as the civilians around me were apt to call it) and I consulted Google about the mysterious C-suite. Ah! It's big-wigs at private-sector companies: CEO, COO, CFO, CIO, CMO ... so many Chiefs that it sounded like the military. When speaking with another transitioning officer, he asked the same vocabulary question. What a relief! I was not alone! The world of business had its own jargon, and I was going to have to learn it.

Having an openness to learning might seem like a common-sense requirement for the military/civilian transition, but it required a philosophy. I certainly didn't know everything I needed to know and, on the outside, would not have a staff to help me think through problems. That's one point you need to consider, especially if you have been privileged to command. When you retire, you don't get to take your staff with you. I sure miss them. You have no idea! I always considered myself open to learning. It was and is a passion of mine, so much so that I can't promise I won't pursue my doctorate in the future. This love of learning helped me during my transition. There was plenty we didn't know in the early days of transition. I would need to talk to lots of people on the outside, near places we desired to live and with skills and backgrounds not military related.

· ·

When you retire, you don't get to take your staff with you. I sure miss them.

· ·

Despite my love of learning, my ego often got in the way when I came upon something I didn't know or understand, which only reinforced the need for a philosophy to guide me. I was a seasoned combat veteran and Army colonel with more than 27 years of experience leading large organizations under the most challenging conditions in the most horrific environments. What did the world outside the gates of my installation have to teach me? Quite a bit, actually, and I needed to swallow my pride and spoon it all up. Sure, I would need to analyze learning opportunities as they presented themselves to see if they were worthy of my time, but I needed to keep an openness to learning. I still do. I've had coffee, lunch and Skype sessions with people far younger than me ... who came to our first conversation with no idea what a Colonel, Bronze Star or UCMJ was. However, they were well-versed in the language of business and the modern corporate workplace.

· ·

I needed to keep an openness to learning. I still do.

· ·

Network — it's a word I've mentioned so many times in this book that you've got to be sick hearing it. But, if you're anything like me, you need to be hit over the head with its new definitions and implications in the civilian world. In the Army, I had all kinds of contexts for the word "network." My network was what I used to execute mission command across my infantry brigade. Or it was the enemy network

I spent the latter half of my career staring down. *No, it's a verb, colonel.* Ah, of course! Time to get out there and "network."

In addition to countless one-on-one meetings, I attended networking events to meet new people and talk about what I was up to. *Speed dating for business,* a friend called it. I took courses (some free, some I paid for), which helped me focus on business development and marketing. And I even hired an author coach to help me with my book-writing aspirations. My network suddenly included all kinds of talented, interesting people, many of whom don't wear a uniform to work.

Early into my transition, I forced myself to be open to all kinds of learning — not just new vocabulary and new perspectives from business professionals. As such, I dug in to learn some new technology and processes too. I discovered and began to use numerous business operating systems and software, like Trello, Slack and HubSpot. I learned a bit about customer relationship management (CRM) and even project management certification, commonly referred to as PMP (Project Management Professional) certification.[1] I met civilians working with complex Knowledge Management systems and applying executive coaching processes to improve people and organizations. I found these programs fascinating and thankfully saw some very clear linkage to my military experience. I discovered programs that put my old-fashioned Microsoft PowerPoint and Excel "Ninja skills" to shame. The military never really had the ability to introduce new operating systems with the speed, innovative and nimble roll-out that private-sector organizations could, and this new space was a great place to learn. And learn I did.

---

1   I never got PMP certified or formally trained on any hip new business systems but it's not a bad idea as you transition. I'm certain such certifications or training programs would teach me a thing or two.

. . . .

Tuck your ego in the breast pocket of your dress uniform and leave it in the closet.

. . . .

Tuck your ego in the breast pocket of your dress uniform and leave it in the closet. The world — and yes, these youngsters — have much to teach us.

LOOKING BACK ...

I can't help but reflect on my time as a squadron commander in Alaska, the year before we deployed. We did more leader training (events that I was required to attend) than at any time in my career to date. And after we had returned from combat, assessing the efficacy of our pre-deployment training, we wished we had done more. Leader training paid off in spades during our year in combat. Looking back, I should have done more learning in my transition. There is surely a video, a course and likely even a book about everything I didn't know in transition. From networking to Google analytics, to business finance, to the roles of C-Suite members and on and on, I should have been more disciplined to study more. It felt weird sitting in some of the classes I did. And some were not as good as I had hoped for but I pulled what I needed from them and it helped. Pick a subject you know little about as you transition and conduct your own leader training. Subscribe to *Forbes* or *Fast Company* while still in uniform. Get in the know!

Chapter 13
CLOSE YOUR EYES AND LEAP

Retire. It's a word I've used more than a hundred times so far in this book, and yet it's still a word that doesn't sit well with me. When I say I'm retired, most people look at me in amazement. — as if to say, "Wow, hit the rocking chair already?" Jim Hughes introduced me to a concept called the "encore career" and that's exactly what I set out to build when I left the Army —my next act in a show that must and will go on. The phrase "encore career: was made popular by Marc Freedman, in his book *Encore: Finding Work That Matters in the Second Half of Life*. An encore career as defined in Wikipedia is the work in the second half of life that combines continued income, greater personal meaning and social impact.[1] Encore careers are what we *want* to do when we're finished doing what we *had* to do. They are not an indictment of the decades of work that preceded them in careers where longevity and loyalty might have been necessary or highly valued, or in careers that can only be conducted with young, strong bodies.

---

1   https://en.wikipedia.org/wiki/Encore_career

Encore careers, in my experience, are incredibly popular among those of us who served in the military, those who worked in the trades or other professions with unions and pensions, and those who were professional athletes, police officers or firefighters. An estimated 4.5 million people between the ages 50 and 70 are already working along encore careers with another 21 million planning to join them soon.[2] Some of these careers are found in non-profit, coaching services and healthcare. At first, "encore career" sounded a lot like another "job" to me, yet I can clearly see a path to fulfillment there. I think I will always do something, even beyond a point in my life when I need a paycheck. Maybe it will be mentoring or speaking pro bono. There will always be a Rob Campbell Encore. Stay tuned! But as for you, how can thinking of your post-military life as your "next act" — your encore — shift your attitude away from fear and uncertainty toward excitement and pride? Coming on stage for an encore is about giving the people more of what they love about you. What are your unique talents, skills and passions, and how can your encore show off the very best of you while providing a truly fulfilling personal experience?

· ·

Coming on stage for an encore is about giving the people more of what they love about you. What are your unique talents, skills and passions, and how can your encore show off the very best of you while providing a truly fulfilling personal experience?

· ·

TO TAKE A KNEE OR TO CLOSE YOUR EYES AND LEAP?

"Take a knee." I had heard this phrase used a lot during my career, conjuring thoughts of when an infantryman takes a knee to keep

---

2   https://www.fidelity.com/viewpoints/retirement/working-in-retirement and
     https://encore.org/

himself relatively out of sight of the enemy, or to pause and rest from long movements over difficult terrain. But what most people in my world have meant when they talk about "taking a knee" is taking a break from a busy, demanding life. We often used the term when we were headed off to one of the Army's mandatory courses, where we were sure to catch some much-needed respite from a loaded military schedule. This phrase came to mind often during my transition journey. It was such a common topic of conversation with others when I'd talk about retiring from the Army that I thought the decision between "taking a knee" or taking a big leap into something new deserved its own chapter in this book.

I always hated the term, frankly, as it meant I would give less than my all. I attended every course I went to in the Army with a special motivation to get the most out of it. Sure, I slowed my pace down and made greater investment, spending time with family, but I never liked the implication of "taking a knee." In the post-military life, I would use this philosophy to help me determine what lifestyle I would assume. It sure had been a demanding 27 years. I confess: I was smoked. But is taking a knee what I desired — to retire to my hammock with my solitaire app open and a few days' growth of facial hair? The sound of it was very inviting. I knew I would have a few months off while on terminal leave, but would I ignore my leave days and sprint toward a job or some other opportunity or would I embrace that time and catch my breath? Hammocks, hair growth and solitaire sounded great, but I did need to think seriously about ending work at this point in my career to pursue a non-job-like activity or, better said, a passion in this encore life. Under my "openness to learning" philosophy, I heard a business mentor insist that "If you love what you do, you'll never have to work a day in your life." This is the Jim Hughes philosophy. I wondered if there was a way to take a leap into something exciting and pride-inspiring, rather than taking a knee? Or maybe doing something that fell somewhere between taking a break and taking a risk.

Passion projects and respite aside, there were financial demands on me. I still needed to educate my youngest son, and Leslie and I had dreams that would need funding. Could I toss the job idea and focus instead on reading, relaxing and hanging out with my wife under a Colonel's pension? Would I *want* to do that?

Many of the retirees I spoke with did take some time off. Some of them quickly learned they could not deal with the space and time and needed something to do. They couldn't find the activity they sought in their own homes so they entered back into the workforce. I had zero experience in this area but wanted to keep my mind open to taking a break. Perhaps my leave period, leading up to my official retirement date, would be a good beta test. Either way, I was not going to "take a knee" and become a turnip, sitting on the couch binge-watching Netflix. And I loved my wife and home and was not one of those disconnected husbands looking for the next opportunity to hang with the guys. I was going to do something productive with my time. The philosophy for me became "do something productive" instead of "take a knee." For you, it might be either or neither; perhaps you'll take a huge leap into something intense and different — like moving to Europe or going to graduate school or opening a restaurant. You don't need to know exactly where you're headed; I certainly didn't. All I knew for sure was that, like some of my peers, I would need something to do. I always will in some form. I am an extrovert and I need social interaction. Moving forward, I knew I would need to feed this "social need" if I elected to do something productive while enjoying these new freedoms I had.

Today, I find myself very busy. My weeks are filled with coffee or beer meetings to meet and network with new people. I'm a visionary and an entrepreneur, so I'm always bursting with new ideas. These ideas take me from network to network, person to person. My wife comments every now and then that I'm as busy as I used to be in the military. Fair comment, but I still own my schedule, which is where

I want to remain. My calendar several weeks from now has lots of white space. I'll fill it for sure between speaking, coaching, consulting and networking events but I'm still at the controls! I love what I do.

LOOKING BACK ...

I didn't leap into the fire (or even another frying pan), but I didn't sit still either. Indeed, I did take a partial knee for a few months in the fall of 2016. I wrote some and networked some but took it easy. I wish I had been introduced to the concept of an encore career earlier in my transition. I found it eventually but it would have been helpful to have more informed encore discussions with Leslie and other trusted friends while still under the security blanket of my active duty paycheck.

Look through the lens of service and personal passion as you contemplate the "what's next" and as you bring definition and clarity (as much as you can) to your encore life and career. Service was easy in uniform and it gave us fulfillment. Your passion was issued to you by the military. Give yourself a break, if you are able. It is very healing. But then find that same fulfillment of service in your encore life and career. Remember there is a blank piece of paper — not a rigid career timeline — placed in front of you. Bust out that government pen you probably have a bunch of and use up that ink, but know that what appears before you is governed only by you and your mate. Imagine, then act.

Chapter 14
CONSIDER YOUR OPTIONS: PERSPECTIVES ON DISABILITY

"Disability," as it's defined by the military, is a tricky topic for many of us. In truth, I have had a hard time with this one and I risk coming off as a hypocrite here. This mini chapter is more in the perspective camp versus a "I suggest you do what I did." I remember having the disability discussion with retirees during my senior years, still on active duty but with retirement as a small blip on my radar. Some were hell-bent on achieving 100%. Some even took pride in the fact that they "won" 100% disability or came close. Others didn't want to deal with it. There were only a few in the middle, like me. I was offered some different, even competing, perspectives on this topic.

Here they are. These are not Rob Campbell philosophies etched in stone. I would not take a hard stand on any of them. Remember I approach this topic with some internal conflict. These are all worthy of debate, with yourself, other trusted people and family. Here I offer my deepest thoughts and reservations. My goal is to inform your own thinking and decision. I don't necessarily agree with the more extreme arguments, on either side of the spectrum.

- The federal funding is there, so use it if you need it. Our federal government allocates funding for military disability, so it is not like they must chase more taxpayer monies to fund it.

- While it is true you volunteered, your nation sought your service in this time of enduring war, even asked of your life in its defense if needed. The military has put you through the wringer in your career. The physical demands were great and came at a cost. You deserve this money.

- Because you volunteered, as the Army Ranger creed states, "fully knowing the hazards of your chosen profession," you are not entitled to disability pay.

- Define disabled. Shouldn't it mean one cannot walk or see or function normally? If that is truly our definition and we use it to gather our pay, many (including myself) do not deserve it.

- The money is not for you. It is for your family members who may have to deal with your disabilities or who, at a minimum, suffered as a result of you being sent to war.

- Disability pay is acceptable for those abilities you lost due to contact with the enemy and/or a related injury from something you may have been ordered to do in training. You deserve pay for those disabilities but nothing else.

- You are still young (50) and your disabilities have not taken hold yet. When you age, they will impact your life, therefore you should accept it now.

- PTSD, while perhaps not prevalent in your current state, will rear its ugly head once on the outside away from the "tribe."

Sebastian Junger, in his book *Tribe*, shares the following specific to disability.[1]

> *"Today's veterans claim three times the number of disabilities that Vietnam veterans did yet experienced a casualty rate roughly one third that of Vietnam ... Part of the problem is bureaucratic: in an effort to speed up access to benefits, in 2010 the Veterans Administration declared that soldiers no longer have to cite an incident — a firefight or roadside bomb — in order to be eligible for disability compensation.... Today disability claims are dominated by tinnitus and PTSD which can be imagined, exaggerated or even faked. A recent investigation by the VA Office of the Inspector General found that the higher a veteran's PTSD disability rating, the more treatment he or she tends to seek until they reach 100% disability at which point treatment visits plummet. Many quit completely."*

This speaks to a generation of veterans who feel entitled. I recall many servicemembers who, in my opinion, used their disability as a crutch or may even have faked it. I'm bothered by veterans like this. They marginalize those who are truly suffering.

All these perspectives outlined above have some merit. I believe you need to find comfort with where you fit. I submitted my medical records to the reviewer during my retirement processing and let him determine what my problems were. I had a look, recalled all the issues I was seen for over the years or health symptoms that still bothered me, and confirmed that he has was right. I could not recall anything else. I did take the sleep apnea test at my wife's urging. Turns out I had it severe. I even used a machine to breathe at night for a short while. I hated it. She has told me that I sleep better now. Perhaps it was job stress. No shortage of that in the military.

---

1   Sebastian Junger, *Tribe: On Homecoming and Belonging*, Twelve, 2016, pp. 88-89.

I do not consider myself disabled. When I use the word disabled, I envision a veteran who is missing a limb, has some extreme dismemberment or another impairment that prevents him or her from leading a normal life. Normal. As I write, I am seeking treatment for nerve damage that's causing pain in my feet and preventing me from running, an activity I enjoy. I can still do low-impact physical fitness activities, which I do. I function quite normally otherwise. I still go to the gym in the morning, even though my workouts are not like they were in the military. This ailment is not listed on my disability claim, nor do I care to add it. My father-in-law did two tours in Vietnam, flying Hueys or Slicks. I know he has experienced more hardship than I, but he has not claimed anything ... nor does he plan to. One part of me wishes he would. The other part admires him for his refusal. He is definitely not the entitlement type. I believe he subscribes to the Ranger Creed.

So here's where I landed on the topic, right or wrong. I submitted my documentation and let the process do its thing. I wound up 60% disabled and I know I can fight for more but I choose not to. I have not filed for PTSD. I feel a tad bit guilty about my disability pay. Perhaps it is my ethical dilemma in this encore life, but I don't lose much sleep over it. Here is why. I can look myself in the mirror and know I did not fake anything. That money helps my family live and my son attend college, so I put it to good use. I'm not one of those dudes you see on videos unable to work yet hiking the Appalachian Trail. Aside from those who have blatantly faked it and are gaming the system, I do not judge those who have chosen differently. This is just where I land.

LOOKING BACK ...

I use caution comparing generations and hardship in war. We have each traveled unique paths and have enjoyed or endured unique journeys. I've always felt that today's veterans stand on the shoulders of those who went before us. We've benefited from more modern equipment, life-saving procedures and better communications. That said, our enemies continue to devise innovative and horrific ways of spilling servicemember blood. I certainly do not feel guilty about my retirement pay. As I say to many like me, "We have already worked a lifetime." I placed my life on the line for my country in three combat tours. That is far more than many other citizens did or would do.

Chapter 15
STAY CONNECTED TO YOUR TRIBE

A Vietnam veteran and dear friend of mine — who served as the honorary colonel of my regiment while I was in brigade command — spoke with my officers once at my request. He had experienced horror in combat as a platoon leader and suffered as a result. I admired his bravery, sharing his story with modern combat veterans or soon-to-be combat veterans. His suffering did not begin until after he had retired after 20 years of service. This stuck with me. His trauma surfaced only after he left his Army tribe behind. While in uniform surrounded by soldiers with shared experiences, he was able to deal with

Lieutenant Colonels Jon Graebener and Dallas Cheatham, both operations officers of Rob's, taking battalion command from each other. Rob and Leslie could not miss this! (Fort Polk, LA, 2019)

this. That stuck with me and I carried it into my transition. While I didn't experience horror on a scale which he did, I brought memories of combat, decisions I made on the battlefield into this next journey. I carried the memory of fallen soldiers with me. I wondered if these things would bother me in the same way after I was away from the tribe.

The power of staying connected to your tribe (and the risk of losing touch with them) is something I feel so strongly about that I speak about it in front of audiences. The first time I delivered a speech entitled "Stay Connected to the Tribe" was at an event hosted by a very generous CEO. It was a baseball game where he gathered several members of the Veterans Treatment Court in North Carolina. This program assisted veterans who had committed minor offenses as a result of their combat trauma. I could not vouch for their cases, nor did I really want to involve myself. They were getting help. I wanted to deliver a message: "Stay connected to the tribe."

When I signed out on terminal leave, I wanted to get away from the Army. I wanted to decompress and immerse myself into a society I had left behind. I loved the Army but didn't want to return. I did keep in contact with several military buddies on social media platforms but that was the extent of it. I found, as I approached the two-year anniversary of my retirement, that I did need to stay connected in some fashion. A friend of mine who leads the Veteran's Affairs department at the local university asked if I wanted to be the vice president for the Association of the United States Army (AUSA) chapter at his university. I thought about it for a few days because I wanted to be sure I could dedicate the proper time to the position and organization, given all my other ventures. I determined that I could but I also saw it as an opportunity to stay connected to the tribe. The position would allow me to remain an ambassador for the Army in my local community and reconnect every now and then.

The special bond we feel as warriors is not one that needs explanation in this book. I have to say that I enjoy the brief moments where I can connect with those who have experienced all that I have. We usually talk about topics other than war, like beer, leadership or sports. It is an act of healing, at its most basic level, and I wanted to give this advice to the veterans at the baseball game. Stay connected to the tribe. I am a tribal member — your brother — if only due to our shared service to our nation. In your next chapter — your encore life and career — take the time you need to place your service behind you, but please find a way to stay connected, in some fashion, to the tribe. You need them, and they need you.

· ·

In your next chapter — your encore life and career — take the time you need to place your service behind you, but please find a way to stay connected, in some fashion, to the tribe. You need them, and they need you.

· ·

I'm spending more and more time thinking about this and visiting this space as my journey continues. My role with AUSA helps in this respect, as does my executive director position with VetToCEO. My friend John, who co-founded VetToCEO, and I connect often over beers and talk about our time in uniform as well as the current state of veteran transition. It's inspirational to me, humorous and healing all at once. I cherish these moments more than I realized when I walked out of the transition center at Fort Carson, Colorado, nearly four years ago. I do all of this on a part-time basis so I'm able to do other things I've committed to, but it is a part of my encore life and career that I want to hold onto for years to come.

I'm pleased to report that several of my friends involve themselves in veteran's affairs in a variety of ways. One is a champion of military spouses, helping them transition into fulfilling careers. Another uses cycling to assemble veterans. Another is involved with the new National Veteran's Memorial and Museum, and another serves with an organization that helps veterans to transition into careers in technology. There are lots of options for staying connected and probably more veterans where you live than you might think. Find the tribe or build it, then return to it often!

LOOKING BACK ...

Reflecting on this, it's interesting to me how my tribe connection unfolded and how I felt about it. I think I needed that divorce from the military following my retirement. It was similar to the feeling I got on active duty when I took off on leave and attempted to shut off the military. Of course, I couldn't then as I can now but I think I needed this space for a while. I'd say it was a little less than a year before I began to miss my tribe. To fill that void, I connected with the veteran offices at the local colleges, wrote a few articles and spoke about veteran issues before a large crowd of business leaders. My interactions in these places opened doors for me, such as my AUSA and MILSPO appointments and the VetToCEO opportunity. I conference call with my VetToCEO brethren each Friday and I feel like I'm back in the rifle squad. It's hilarious and

Post-retirement at Fort Gordon, GA, watching LTC Jay Harty, one of Rob's former officers, taking command of soldiers. Rob and Leslie had zero responsibility there, other than watching with pride.

enormously satisfying all at once. These interactions, coupled with a greater desire to return to military installations to witness the achievements of former soldiers of mine, have filled my cup. When the timing is right for you, start to expand your Facebook network with former warriors. Pick up the phone and reconnect with them as I have done. Find the places where veterans hang out and pay a visit to see if it's a fit. Whatever you choose, do not overlook the benefits of staying connected to your tribe. They get you and care about you like few others do.

Chapter 16
KEEP UP ON YOUR PT

Stay in shape! It's in our DNA, and the importance of PT to our military lives was too big to be forgotten after we transition into a civilian world. I'm definitely not in the same shape I was back when I was in the military. I could, however, probably muscle my way through an Army PT test and pass, but guess what? Nobody cares! It seems my entire career was dominated by alternating cycles — periods of peace when I had recently completed the PT test and had some time to relax and alter my program, and periods of tension when my angst would build up as the next test approached. I always did very well at the PT test, so I really had no reason to worry. I don't know what my problem was. A good fear perhaps? One that kept me honest and physically fit? I have to say that the thought of never having to take that dreaded test again is very pleasing, especially now that they changed it. I believe this gives me shit-talking rights. "I served when the PT test was hard!" Of course, I can utter those words but never have to back it up!

I always felt judged by peers and the Army for my level of physical fitness, as if no matter how fit I was, it was never quite good enough. I ran two marathons, achieved top scores on my PT tests and could bench-press more than 225 pounds. I was not the fastest runner.

I could hold my own but there were always the fast runners, many of whom I worked for, who tended to take pride or bravado in their fitness levels and judged me for not being able to meet their standards. It's nice to say goodbye to that.

How you care for your body and your health after your transition to a civilian life is deeply personal. Here is what I do. I still get up at 5:00 a.m. Some think I'm insane for this but I'm one who needs to get my PT in early. I won't get to it during the day and if I miss a workout, guilt sets in. Yes, I carried that guilt with me into this new chapter of my life. I like it. It keeps me honest. I've seen some who, upon retirement, let themselves go. I have a lot of living left to do, and I need a healthy body to do it.

One of the best things about post-military life is that *we* can determine what our PT test is. And you don't have to answer to anyone but yourself. I use elliptical machines and free weights in the gym. I cannot run currently because of my feet, but I am working on that. I would like to start running again. I will probably buy a bike and alter my program a bit so I can avoid a fitness plateau. There are days where my schedule is empty but I still enjoy getting up early and getting the most out of the day. Early days are one of the things I still enjoy and am glad to keep at it.

Figure out what you enjoy. If running is not it, then stop. Play racquetball or another sport that makes you break a sweat. A friend of mine started yoga. Us infantrymen

A new kind of PT – post-retirement "field training!" Rob at the beach (Topsail Island, NC, 2018).

used to laugh at programs like that but yoga is really great. I've done yoga with my wife. Maybe join a spin class or try Tai Chi. Put your service in your past but carry forward that voice of the guy with the whistle who can bark in your ear every now and then and tell you to quick slacking!

LOOKING BACK ...

Looking back, I'm satisfied with my loyalty to physical fitness. I still like to get it done in the morning but I've shifted a bit. On days that aren't so busy, I might sleep in and PT just before lunch. I wish I had treated some of my ailments earlier, like my feet ... which still prevent me from running. I'll get them fixed eventually but I miss the relative ease and responsiveness of healthcare while on active duty. Take my advice and get all patched up before bidding farewell. Leslie and I have experimented with plant-based diets and Keto. It's been fun but challenging at times. We own our schedule so we can better control when, where and what we eat. My greatest pearl of wisdom is to treat PT similar to charting your course. Cast aside the military PT score card and start with a blank sheet of paper. Most importantly, put something down on that paper and follow it.

Chapter 17
CONSIDER ENTREPRENEURSHIP

Allow me to introduce you to a term we rarely used on the military: *entrepreneurship.* "Entrepreneurial" may have slipped into our lexicon a time or two to describe someone or some event (i.e., someone or something that was fresh and new and enterprising), but "innovative" seemed to be the choice word instead. Entrepreneurship implies a business startup, which we did not engage in while serving (though we started up initiatives and built camps on foreign soil), and it implies a sole founder — or two or three partners — creating something from scratch. Our "business" (the Army, in my case, but also the Navy, Air Force, Marines and Coast Guard) predates us by hundreds of years. Through innovation, we made improvements to it. But we never owned it and we never led it, though we led significantly within it.

However you define it, entrepreneurship can be an intriguing concept to those of us leaving the military in search of what's next. To this old soldier, being an entrepreneur is about launching a new and different private business venture or a positive disruption to the status quo to create a product or service that is better. When I hear the term "entrepreneur," I envision a person or two with a great idea and the energy and drive to bring it forth. Uber, Airbnb, DoorDash and Pinterest come to mind when I think of entrepreneurship, not the 5th Bomb Wing or the 101st Airborne Division. My Army peers and I never gave it much thought to being entrepreneurial — to building a better mouse trap or trouncing the competition or scaling up for an initial public offering. We didn't have to. Our "business" was never going out of "business."

· ·

My Army peers and I never gave it much thought to being entrepreneurial — to building a better mouse trap or trouncing the competition or scaling up for an initial public offering. We didn't have to. Our "business" was never going out of "business."

· ·

That said, I've always thought of myself as an alternative thinker. Indeed, I struggled with conventional warfare most of my career yet took to asymmetric warfare or counterinsurgency quite naturally. I was a disruptor. I took on the old traditional ways of warfare to develop something better. Iraq and Afghanistan were my beta tests for this disruption. We were getting it wrong, not achieving desired effects, and our methods and mindset needed to change. I hit resistance. The big, traditional Army pushed back. Once transitioned in my civilian life, though, I could disrupt all I wanted. Entrepreneurial perhaps? You be the judge.

Once I was retired, I thrust myself into entrepreneurial networking events. There I interacted with people much younger than me: venture capitalists, entrepreneurs, Millennials in t-shirts, flip-flops and man-buns trying out new concepts and hunting for funds to support their ideas. It felt quite out-of-body for me. In fact, the whole journey of entrepreneurship, while attractive, felt quite foreign. As

I crossed into the veteran transition space, I interacted with organizations promoting veteran entrepreneurship or "vetrepreneurship." These organizations were working extra hard, struggling to attract and keep veterans on entrepreneurial journeys. It made me think and reflect on my own entrepreneurship ... writing a book and starting a business from my beach home. I recalled the struggles I experienced when trying to develop a client avatar, a unique value proposition and find someone to pay me for what I could deliver.

WHY COMBAT VETERANS LACK THE COURAGE FOR ENTREPRENEURSHIP

Veterans, especially those who have served in combat, can be characterized by their courage, tenacity and extreme dedication to mission accomplishment. Indeed, it seems oxymoronic to use *lack of courage* and *combat veteran* in the same sentence, as I have done in the heading above. Most believe, with good reason, that these courageous warriors are the perfect candidates to start a business and fuel the American economy. Afterall, many Fortune 500 companies were founded by veterans. I've heard it said that fewer than 5% of post-9/11 veterans have started their own business ventures, and I'm not really surprised by that number. Maybe those of us who are used to having had budgets for equipment and people are turned off by how difficult it is for a guy or a gal with a great idea to get funding for a new business. And surely most of us come out the other side of our military/civilian transition without a great mentor to help us think like business owners. Add to that the extreme focus on "how to get a job" in military transition programs, and you have a perfect recipe for veterans who are highly likely to choose a traditional job or a hammock. But I believe that, amidst all of this, there is something else at play: fear.

As you well know, danger and military service are synonymous regardless of service or MOS. Let's consider this example: Visit the 82nd Airborne Division at Fort Bragg, North Carolina, and you will witness thousands of servicemembers engaged in

*On parade, 82nd Airborne Division
(Fort Bragg, NC, 2005).*

risky parachute operations almost daily. If they are not parachuting from the sky, you will find them training with live ammunition in very close proximity to one another honing their skills for the modern battlefield. The same holds true for our elite special operations servicemembers who train for and conduct operations replete with danger. Place these men and women in combat where targets shoot back and the danger multiplies. While courage is a prerequisite for service in the military, it must be viewed through a different lens if we are to understand why entrepreneurship scares off warriors. When viewed through three optics — a culture of risk-aversion, a loss of human connection and teamwork, and a foreign language — this breakdown in courage is easier to understand. And it happens no matter which branch of the U.S. military you served.

A CULTURE OF RISK-AVERSION

Recall how serious you took your duty to care for America's sons and daughters. Because of the inherent danger of military operations, units create lengthy spreadsheets and briefings to identify risks and implement measures to mitigate them. Risk assessments are a part of practically every military event, such as physical training, parachute operations and even a military ball. It is common, even in the most routine operations, that several levels of approval must be sought for operations to take place. Remember your unit safety officer or the safety office on your installation? These people were everywhere, from operations to training and even in combat. Few military members enter a weekend or a vacation without some form of safety briefing first, and frequently take part in what is called a "safety stand-down" where on-duty and off-duty accident awareness and safety measures are emphasized and trained.

Even in combat, we delayed operations for days or weeks to ensure conditions — like favorable weather to allow aviation support — were optimal and risk was mitigated to minimal levels. This concentration on safety and risk mitigation can be boring and frustrating to troops eager to start their weekend or kick off an important operation, but it works. According to a 2018 Congressional Research Service study, combat casualties have dropped significantly over the years and while casualties from training ebb and flow, they remain substantially low.[1] Measures meant to keep casualties to a minimum are always a good thing. They do, however create a culture of risk-aversion where risk mitigation is a part of every operation, every discussion and on the mind of every servicemember. This creates a mindset that is hard to change once you hang up the uniform to pursue an encore life and career.

Entrepreneurship is void of the extensive risk assessment and safety-focused process found in the military. Good entrepreneurs analyze risk for sure, but not typically on par with military operations. Often, they take risks and even gamble based on a hunch or a great idea. Risks and hazards are often ill-defined or unknown. While products and services can be beta tested to determine business survival, these tests may not paint a full risk picture. There is no "chain of command" or readily available group of experts to examine and approve risk assessments before undertaking activities. Urgency

---

1   https://fas.org/sgp/crs/natsec/RL32492.pdf

can often prohibit a proper analysis and mitigation of risk factors and there are no safety officers to whisper in the ears of entrepreneurs alerting them of dangers they cannot see. And, let's face it, most businesses started by entrepreneurs can afford to take some risks because no matter what goes wrong in their company, there are no body bags. It's a whole new way of thinking.

LOSS OF HUMAN CONNECTION AND TEAMWORK

Aversion to risk isn't the only thing that keeps a lot of veterans from starting our own businesses. Entrepreneurship, at least at first, can be incredibly lonely … and for those of us who are used to being part of that "tribe" I keep talking about, loneliness is hard. In training and in combat, we were never alone. From the very first day in uniform and throughout our careers, the "buddy system" was in effect. Try going anywhere, even to the bathroom in Navy Seal training or in Army basic training, and you are likely to experience some form of punishment, maybe even separation. Remember?

This buddy or team system endures in a team-like profession throughout one's service. Picture a servicemember in full combat gear on a remote battlefield. While the image may show only the servicemember, within arm's reach you'll find their battle buddy. Beyond that exists a larger cohesive team, trained and prepared to come to their rescue. Not in view, but not far away, a helicopter stands ready to spin its blades and extract this servicemember from danger. A forward medical facility is ready to react in seconds to save his or her life. Artillery tubes are pointed toward their battleground ready to provide suppressive fire in a pinch. Unmanned full-motion video aircraft may hover overhead, depicting danger beyond view. Attack aviation and Air Force aircraft patrol the area, ready to swoop in and save the day. The servicemember wears the most modern state-of-the art protective equipment, carries a weapon he or she has been trained extensively to use and is prepared (as are his or her buddies) to administer lifesaving first aid. Other servicemembers, ones he or she has never met, will put their life on the line for them. This, they are sure of. While dangerous and scary, the servicemember is emboldened by an extensive safety net of protection, backed by a team of people who know and trust one another.

Now picture that same servicemember engaged in entrepreneurship then scan left and right and you'll find no one. It is here, in entrepreneurship, the servicemember finds himself or herself alone. This is more than a little jarring for most of us. Some of you lived on aircraft carriers or on bases with thousands of other servicemembers. Love it or hate it, the group was our identity (we even dressed alike!). Once removed from service, however — from this comprehensive safety net and sense of security — trust and teamwork all but vanishes. An investor will not rush to the aid of an entrepreneur should they stumble and fall (which is why veterans require a deep dive on funding options so they can gain familiarity and acumen in this foreign space). A business mentor won't be at arm's length and there will be nothing hovering overhead to detect threats beyond one's view. Their new body armor may only be an email address or a business card from a person who may or may not rush to their aid. This isolation and nakedness generate a new kind of fear, one very foreign to a combat veteran.

A FOREIGN LANGUAGE

Because so few Americans serve in the military, we veterans feel isolated after transition into a society that admires but doesn't understand us. (This truth was a big motivator behind my decision to write this book.) The transition experience, for some, is akin to being thrust into a foreign country ignorant of the local language and customs. In my tours in Iraq and Afghanistan, I felt anxious because I didn't speak the language. I would pick up key Arabic phrases but my trusty interpreter gave me comfort, helping overcome this significant barrier. Entrepreneurship is like this, but usually without the interpreter. It begins with the word entrepreneurship, which is not used in the military, and it snowballs from there. Almost in an instant, money and its associated language becomes the new lexicon of the veteran entrepreneur. Profitability, scale, venture capital and valuation replace phase line, time on target, and mission command. These new words can be spoken, but understanding and embracing them is a foreign experience. It takes time, just like it took time to learn military jargon. It also requires a willingness to feel like a fish out of water.

Money becomes priority number one if you're running a business and are solely responsible for generating your own paycheck. In the military, we certainly were good stewards of our government budgets but rarely, if ever, was money a central issue. As a commander, I had a budget officer or CFO but I rarely ever heard from him or her. We would question a mission's feasibility and effectiveness. We would ask if the commander's intent was understood or if there were sufficient forces for the tasks. We would analyze and mitigate risk. In entrepreneurship, the central question is, can we afford this? Will it create revenue? Is it fundable? Military units don't go out of business, ever. I never lost sleep over my ability to meet payroll. Finances never stood in our way, especially after 9/11 — when the military seemed to operate from a blank government check. I assure you, in the Osama bin Laden raid, there were no dollar signs on the briefing charts.

· ·

As a commander, I had a budget officer or CFO but I rarely ever heard from him or her. We would question a mission's feasibility and effectiveness. We would ask if the commander's intent was understood or if there were sufficient forces for the tasks. We would analyze and mitigate risk. In entrepreneurship, the central question is, can we afford this? Will it create revenue? Is it fundable?

· ·

MAKING ENTREPRENEURSHIP VIABLE FOR VETERANS

If communities and economies are to reap the benefits of veteran-owned businesses — if we desire veterans to become entrepreneurs — we must address the fear, reduce the obstacles and appreciate the mindset shifts necessary for our mutual success. Artillery tubes and attack aviation must be replaced with engaged former military and civilian business mentors akin to the sergeants who used to teach, guide and discipline us. This means persons trusted by the veteran to share knowledge, skills and experience and to challenge them to succeed in their journey. It requires a rhythm of check-ins, reviews of progress and teaching. Though they may be beyond "battle buddy" reach, an effective mentor ought to be a 24-hour lifeline to a veteran as they navigate the obstacles of the entrepreneurial battlefield. Enduring means mentoring continues as long as needed. A successful mentorship journey would only end when phone calls and meetings taper off because the veteran is more comfortable and confident in their entrepreneurship role. If you have already dipped your toe in the business pool, consider how you can benefit from a mentor ... and/or how you can mentor another transitioning servicemember who is considering entrepreneurship instead of another "job."

Having read this book as far as you have, you know I'm a believer in lifelong learning, and my philosophies around this apply to those transitioning services members considering entrepreneurship too. Education must be the new body armor of the veteran entrepreneur. A short class on how to create a business plan won't cut it. It must be comprehensive and geared toward overcoming this fear. The language of business must be presented in ways a veteran can translate and understand without the assistance of an interpreter. Skilled teachers must present risk management through a new lens. Vignettes of successful and unsuccessful entrepreneurs should be shared, along with exercises that expose veterans to new methods of thinking about and managing risk. Mentors should challenge and embolden veterans to muster the courage they found in combat in this new space. Much like intelligence officers provided details on enemy forces, so too should educators provide intelligence and instruction on the multiple paths within entrepreneurship, such as start-up, franchise or an owner-financed business purchase.

. . . .

Education must be the new body armor of the veteran entrepreneur.

. . . .

My friend John really opened my eyes to the franchise option of entrepreneurship. It is what we did in our careers. Think about it. A franchise is an existing organization — which typically comes with an established brand, market, history and existing structure. You simply take it over and follow the rules (I'm simplifying a bit, but follow me). In the military, we took charge of existing organizations already functioning, equipped and manned. Even with the establishment of a new unit, it followed an existing template. There are so many striking parallels when you examine it further, yet becoming a franchisor is spoken of very little in military transition programs and veteran entrepreneurship accelerators. I think that's a huge opportunity missed.

Lastly, the journey of veteran entrepreneurship ought to be addressed as just that — a journey. Many veteran entrepreneurship programs, while well-intentioned, are not comprehensive enough. All servicemembers are welcomed regardless of whether they're a good fit and, after their focused time in a program, they are left to "go it alone." But we must remember that veterans aren't natural loners ... we thrive on the tribe.

Combat veterans fought for the very freedom entrepreneurship provides. We ought to enjoy what we fought for. Equipped and emboldened by a new approach to risk, new civilian comrades and entrepreneurial language skills, we can muster the courage to climb that first steep mountain then stay on course to become America's next generation of business owners. It is my hope that readers of this book will keep in touch, and I'm particularly interested in learning about your business ventures and how I can support and celebrate you. Hooah!

LOOKING BACK ...

I remain an advocate for entrepreneurship and always will. Chasing an idea you deeply believe in is passion-alignment at its best. I stuck with it partly because I am stubborn and felt that walking away would be a violation of who I truly was. I felt I would betray the values and courage the Army instilled in me if I didn't give this effort at least a few years to bear fruit. The journey was and is anything but easy and I continue to ponder jumping into something more predictable and fruitful. Perhaps there is a better way. Perhaps I should have gotten a job to bring in some money while chipping away at my leadership business. Those of us with a pension (a vanishing benefit in today's world) possess what I believe to be a distinct advantage. The bottom will not fall out. You will have a steady, albeit small, paycheck coming each month and it will come without fail. I know that helps me sleep better.

Chasing an idea you deeply believe in is passion-alignment at its best.

Entrepreneurship can be what you want it to be. You can build a little company or a big company. You can be a one-person company that does a little or a lot. You can be a year-round business or a seasonal business that allows you to travel and take long vacations. You can work from home or lease an office or storefront. Whatever you do, if you choose entrepreneurship, I hope you'll remember that you don't have to kill yourself in the journey. While I had some restless nights, I didn't lose hair or start smoking or drinking to kill my start-up stress.

And you don't even have to choose between being your own boss and having a boss — you can do both. You can balance a traditional full-time or part-time job with an entrepreneurial passion (a side gig, if you will) in your early days after retirement … as a way to explore ideas you may have had but could not act on while in uniform. Believe me — there are several paths to entrepreneurship and you have incredible power and flexibility, if you seek both control and a loosening of the rigor you became accustomed to in the armed forces. Even if you've never pictured yourself as a business person, it's an idea worth exploring, even if only casually and noncommittally at first.

If you decide to commit to an entrepreneurial venture, know that you can do this! Face the fear and pursue an idea with a vengeance. Be your own boss and command your own calendar. I've found it to be very fulfilling, and you might too.

Chapter 18
SELL YOUR SHIT AND DOWNSIZE

There we were. Yup, you guessed it. We sold the beloved beach house. I *told* you we didn't know how not to PCS every two to three years, and were likely to force *ourselves* to move a few times in this new encore life! So we did. A little more than two years after leaving the Army and starting our new lives on the beach in Topsail Island, North Carolina, we decided it was time for a change.

Let me back up. There we were. It was probably around 9:00 p.m., our new "old people" bedtime. (I can't last much longer these days, especially as I continue to fight aging at 5:00 a.m. with daily, self-imposed workouts.) Leslie and I were chatting about life and finances, and I was trying to hammer home a point about why we should sell the house and downsize. So I made a hand gesture like a graph showing how our income was sure to grow ... but so too was our debt and/or expenses with the home improvements we desired (and home repairs that were sure to come). Add to this the fact that we were currently paying for more property than we needed, because we had purchased the adjacent beach lot to prevent another home being built on it. With my hand and forearm forming a straight line angling up at 45 degrees, I formed the income growth line. My other arm formed the same upward angle just below the other. This arm represented our debt and expenses. Then I dropped my lower arm to show a downward angle where I wanted our debt and expenses to be — upward on income, downward on debt and expenses. We have a winner! That's when the lightbulb lit up for both of us. While we had been skating around the topic for some time, that's the visual we both needed. It was time to "cut sling load," as I might have said in the Army — time to rid ourselves of the house, much of our dust-collecting stuff, and the adjacent lot ... and PCS!

At this point, we were about two and a half years into our mortgage. My business was showing signs of promise, as was Leslie's, but we were not in the "crushing it" phase yet. Leslie and I had talked a few times since buying the house about "selling it all" and living a nomadic lifestyle. These conversations could get contentious, I believe because we were emotionally invested in our home and our belongings. We usually ended with convincing ourselves we were crazy and we let the topic drop. Afterall, she finally had her large studio, the "Raven's Nest" — each corner filled with a different creation — and I had my office, the "Eagle's Nest" — adorned from floor to ceiling with my military bling. Not to mention two guest rooms, a garage full of tools, my motorcycle, kayaks and other island gear, and six outdoor patios ... including a widow's walk where you could see both the ocean and the Atlantic Intercoastal Waterway. It was a cool pad with plenty of room for entertaining, storing our decades' worth of collected stuff and enjoying the beach, 244 steps from our front door. Of course, even with all this space, we spoke about renting a storage unit for our "stuff." My garage was not climate-controlled and anything down there tended to mold in the intense North Carolina humidity.

A NEW KIND OF FREEDOM

A new kind of freedom — beyond what I was already enjoying —was calling me and I could not ignore it. Jim Hughes and I spoke often and I was envious of the experiences he was having: country-hopping and utterly free from the expenses and headaches of cable, electric, home warranty, water, sewer, trash, gym membership and property taxes. I despised these payments and thought often about living only off our retired pay, navigating the globe from wondrous spot to wondrous spot. I still do. Add to this new kind of wanderlust the institutional effects of 27 years of service, which were still alive in both of us. The feelings we were having and the thoughts we pondered were akin to the military life we led for almost three decades — the excitement that would build a few years into an assignment, eager to learn of where the military would send us next. While frequent PCS'ing was part of the reason we retired, it was still in our DNA. This, we came to realize, was not a bad thing.

As the months and years went by, the voice inside became louder. I couldn't ignore it anymore. I would watch TED Talks where speakers would share their experiences downsizing and I'd find myself asking why we couldn't do such a thing. Leslie and I would look around the house and think about our possessions, most of which we rarely used. Spare bedrooms saw guests only a few times a year, while we heated and air conditioned them and outfitted them with cable TV year-round. As our extended family grew (i.e., as our sons broadened their lives with spouses and/or children), they would rent their own homes during summer vacation. Getting our current dream home into dream condition was a heavy lift. We had yet to furnish many of the outside spaces of the house, and I had lofty ideas for driveway extensions, lighted walkways and a climate-controlled garage. The home was built in the late 1980s yet very well constructed and in great shape. That said, much of it was original construction and needed upgrades. I wanted to change out every door handle, replace all the flooring and redo the kitchen completely. The list went on. I had been a real warrior and now I was what the home improvement stores called a "weekend warrior."

The big picture was more daunting than liberating. Leaving now was a way to proverbially "quit while we were ahead" (though you know I don't like being a "quitter" of any kind). We were facing the better part of a 30-year mortgage and numerous home upgrades. We had survived Hurricanes Matthew and Florence unscathed. We did enjoy our sanctuary and people admired our home when they walked by or came in for a visit. Our neighbors were great and the peace and quiet of the off-season at the beach was blissful. The house, we believed, was in one of the best spots on the island. Its new owners would love it, as we had. Though it had been a short chapter in our lives, it was a wonderful one that soothed the soul, and now it was time to go.

Our sons were beginning their lives — one in Germany and another six hours away in Asheville, North Carolina. It was unlikely they would choose to live nearby. Sure, they might love the beach house someday, but the road there had big dollar signs attached to it. Moreover, it was experiences — not homes — we cherished the most. We had lived in some great houses, mind you, but I can't think of one I would want to return to. We desired experiences more than stuff. So Leslie and I engaged in deep conversation about what we truly needed. Her art posed a difficult challenge, as she had collected quite a bit. And I had a lot of military gear, and it filled up every nook and cranny of our house. We always came back to this one truth: when it came to our collections of "stuff," we never touched them or used them or even looked at much of what we owned. We probably would not miss it. It was scary. There was a life — so many memories — behind all our possessions. From favored furniture pieces to old books, practically everything in our house came with a story from the far reaches of the world. But the stories could survive even without the objects, and we knew it.

. . . .

We always came back to this one truth: when it came to our collections of "stuff," we never touched them or used them or even looked at much of what we owned.

. . . .

MOVIN' ON UP

Leslie and I were always enamored by urban living. I always joked that I wanted to have a loft apartment above an Irish pub so I could walk down and enjoy a Guinness served by my bar tender BFF. And we had recently fallen in love with downtown Wilmington, North Carolina. It had such a great vibe, especially the historic district along the banks of the Cape Fear River, with great restaurants and a laid-back, coastal-town feel. I had several clients in town and was there several days a week, which meant a 45-minute one-way trip from Topsail Island. Though the commute to Wilmington was nothing compared to what one might experience in Washington, DC, it was wearing on me and it felt like "a job." I enjoyed working and networking in Wilmington but waiting for me back on the island was a needy home. The constant attention demanded by that needy, beautiful house was attention we wanted to invest in other places. So we decided to move to the city.

The angst of selling the house was soon replaced by the excitement of a new space and a new community. We began to look at loft apartments in Wilmington and soon found one built in an old factory. The floors were old distressed concrete and the original brick walls and rusty metal girders were still exposed, giving it that picturesque, magazine feel. We found a 1-bedroom, 1.5-bath loft apartment with a nice patio facing the road and shops, and we fell in love. It was a spectacular downsizing math problem. How do you go from 2,400 square feet down to about 1,100? We had collected more than

17,000 pounds of household goods in our years in the military. It wasn't going to fit. It was liberating!

We would list our house for sale as "furnished," which is customary with beach homes, and we started making a list of what we would keep, sell or leave behind. I called our real estate agent, we told our family and off we went. The home sold in 14 days. The lot next door sold a few months later. We made a small profit on both and walked away from the pressure of home debt. We felt an instant sense of relief, coming out from under that burden, and embraced the excitement about our next chapter.

We rented a 10 x 10 climate-controlled storage unit for those items we could not part with, we kept a bed and some favored furniture pieces, and we bid farewell to the rest. Leslie rented studio space across the street from our loft, where she enjoys networking with other artists. I am an enviable commute (about a mile!) from most of my clients and now have the freedom to network more. Hell, I've even come home for a nap some days! From our apartment, we can walk to the gym, yoga studio, several bars and restaurants, a beauty salon and an eyeglass shop, and there's a trolley that takes us into the heart of town. I cut no grass, sweep no driveway, fix no appliances and repair no roofs. It's wonderful. The best part? When the PCS itch comes again, as it surely will, we can cancel our lease, move our much-smaller pile of stuff and take off on another adventure. We are both striving to have the kinds of careers that allow us to live wherever we choose and PCS when we want.

. . . .

I cut no grass, sweep no driveway, fix no appliances and repair no roofs. It's wonderful.

. . . .

BEWARE THE ANCHORS

Following that story, let me plant a seed. I use that anchor title often when coaching transitioning veterans and here's what it means. Accommodate me, if you will, for a little professional theft. I stole "drop anchor" from a Naval officer. He used it to bring pause to the room when he wanted everyone's attention or to spend time on an important topic. To drop anchor quite obviously means to slow or stop the movement of a ship for a specific reason. The more anchors you drop, the harder it is to recover them ... especially over time because they sink further and further into the mud. With respect to transition from military service, anchors come in many forms — your anchors might be the purchase of a home, the commitment of savings dollars to a new venture or splurge, or a new, full-time job that is location-dependent. Anchors, as I'm speaking of them here, are big, heavy decisions and commitments that are not easy to alter or reverse. Take it from this soldier, as I approach four years since retirement, be cautious not to drop too many anchors.

Your military career was quite predictable. Of course, you were going to move from base to base and job to job, but you always knew there would be a house, job security and a lifestyle that you could jettison when the next set of orders arrived. My family and I cherished our life in the military, moving from place to place. But as our children grew and our household belongings amassed, the novelty wore off. With a grateful salute and fond farewell, we were thrust into the ocean of the unpredictable. We would trade predictability and familiar military communities for the abyss, a society we had grown apart from after decades of service. And in the abyss, it's natural to want to anchor or ground yourself to something. That grounding is, in part, why we bought the beach house.

Whether you've been planning your transition for only a short time, or if you've separated from service already and are trying to settle into a "new normal," you know that transition is a period of wonder, fear and emotions. I confess that, at first, Leslie and I felt entitled. We had served and sacrificed for our military and our nation, and we felt entitled to all the riches of our new world. I'd venture to say we were even somewhat bitter — as if we were held back from something that should have been ours long ago, such as stability and a home we could paint and alter as we wished. I was 50 years old and just now starting to enjoy the simple pleasures and freedoms that most civilians had known since they graduated college. We began to script a story of our post-military life, one that fit our preconceived notions and fed our current emotions. We thought it was time to drop anchor, so we bought a house. You now know how that turned out.

So at the risk of a broken record, let me say it to you again: Beware the anchors. Be cautious of making a *permanent* decision (about a house, job, car, community, etc.) to address a *temporary* problem (emotions, entitlement, aspirations of a lofty salary, etc.). Indeed, there will be demands — such as children in school or an existing mortgage — that will steer you but I encourage you to do your best to think long-term, remain flexible and know that you will change.

. . . .

Beware the anchors. Be cautious of making a permanent decision (about a house, job, car, community, etc.) to address a temporary problem (emotions, entitlement, aspirations of a lofty salary, etc.).

. . . .

LOOKING BACK ...

In retrospect, I've learned a lot about downsizing, decluttering and being more thoughtful about "dropping anchors." But I have no major regrets. Settled into our new urban lifestyle in Wilmington, Leslie and I remark to each other almost daily just how wonderful it is. Free from a mortgage and all the trappings of home ownership, we're happy. I know better, of course, than to think we will never buy a house again. We've learned not to close any doors. But as for our last relocation decision? So far, so good.

I have learned to be careful not to drop any anchors. And looking back, I realize that immediately after my departure from the Army, we may have been better served to rent a home, take temporary jobs and/or scale back on financial commitments to allow for the adjustment. Perhaps we could have placed our household goods in storage in order to navigate the transition period and assimilate to new environments. We've even discussed buying a motorhome to free ourselves from our financial commitments and have even *more* freedom to roam.

As I shared with you earlier in this book, a friend told me that it takes a few years to de-institutionalize from service, moving beyond traditional routines and civilianizing our language. My wife and are still in that phase. To some degree, I suspect my sons are still coping with this too. And I'm not sure when it will end. But none of us is apt to sit with our heads in our hands, deeply regretting the decisions we have made since I hung up my uniform in 2016. There are many commitments or anchors I'm quite proud of, and mindset shifts I'm grateful to have made. I love wearing shorts and flip-flops, and I enjoy making my own schedule. All things considered, we are pleased with our encore life and excited about the future.

Chapter 19
CARE FOR YOURSELF – REFLECTIONS ON HEALTH AND WELFARE

I would be remiss if I wrapped up this book without addressing health and welfare. I must confess that I overlooked it in my own transition. I think most servicemembers do because new or worsening health and welfare issues often don't begin (or become obvious) until well after we have departed service. My issues began around the six-month mark of my journey, after my retired pay settled in and my leave days expired. Even then, I could not formally grasp what was happening to me. It took a few years frankly. It continues today.

Only recently have I come to realize the importance of a conscious, deliberate approach to health and welfare as part of transition. And it's on me. I cannot hand health and welfare to my brigade staff for completion by close of business. I cannot expect those around me to adjust because I am dealing with something and I cannot exercise, drink or medicate myself through it (though I understand that some people might try). I don't feel that I am suffering like others I know and read about. I've had my high highs and my low lows, but have come out of each of them OK. I've not slipped into long bouts of depression or anger, though I've had tough days. I've not gone off the deep end with addiction or other reckless behavior. This said, I *have* experienced all of these, save for overdrinking and reckless behavior.

I have felt and grappled with many emotions:

- There have been times in my post-Army life when I felt depressed because my business was not taking off as I desired or when money was tight and bills began to stack up.

- I've struggled with finding a new identity. That identity-crafting was previously done for me in the Army with that big eagle I wore on my uniform.

- I've doubted myself in this new "civilian" space because I once could solve the most challenging battlefield problems, only to discover years later that I can't as easily make people line up for my consulting and speaking services.

- I've been resentful of anyone in the leadership space, especially civilians who were not tested as I was.

- While I don't suffer from chronic or devastating regret about anything, I do look back with some measure of regret over decisions made, both while in uniform and during my transition journey, all of which I have been able to overcome.

My wife, Leslie, remains my confidante and rock through the transition. We communicate often about things that bother us, and we read articles and books (and watch TED Talks and other videos) to bolster our emotional well-being and keep us grounded and at peace. Late in the production of this book I stumbled across two profound books: *Transitioning from Service: The Mental Health Handbook for Transitioning Veterans* by former Green Beret Eric Burleson and *Beyond the Military: A Leader's Handbook for Warrior*

Integration by Lieutenant Colonel (Retired) Jason Roncoroni and Dr. Shauna Springer.

I first found Eric Burleson on LinkedIn. His post, shared by another LinkedIn connection of mine, showcased his book. Knowing I wanted to address this in my book and better equip myself to help other veterans (including myself), I reached out to Eric. He and I spoke only briefly but in that short conversation I took away something deep and thoughtful: *I had experienced trauma.* My most recent trauma was not borne of a horrific firefight, an IED explosion or a battlefield injury. Rather, I had undergone an overnight transition unlike any I had previously experienced. Throughout my entire adult life, Leslie and I (and our kids) had lived in small, safe, isolated military communities. But after my retirement from the Army, we moved to a place far removed from anything militarily familiar and, because of my decades of service, according to Eric, the neurons in my brain had "wired together" to form patterns in my thought process to address everything as an Army infantry colonel, not a civilian. Eric continued (in rapid fashion), explaining that many of the neural pathways my brain had worn in my military life simply didn't work in the life I now lived. He aptly described it as walking along the banks of a creek bed, working harder not to slip into the well-worn center. My brain was working harder, which was causing stress and I had failed to understand it.

In *Transitioning from Service*, Eric helps combat and non-combat veterans of all ages achieve a healthier transition. His approach begins with the need to "stop the bleeding" — dealing with the fresh trauma in the weeks and months following transition. In my transition experience, there was no program or person to highlight this for me. I needed my sergeant. We all had them in the military. Those professional, world-class noncommissioned officers who kept us marching straight and who were equipped with that special radar, alerting them to our struggles. He was not there. Eric's book filled part of that void. I just stumbled upon it late.

Later in the book, Eric suggests we then "reassess, triage, continue basic care," helping ourselves to become more emotionally intelligent, manage grief and differentiate. This battlefield casualty treatment methodology is a perfect analogy for a veteran in transition. Eric proposes group conversation — or, at a minimum, focused conversation with a trusted person — as well as journaling to help. Lastly, Eric guides veterans on how to "cultivate long-term health" by being mindful of physical health, work, relationships and values in a sustained approach to overall health. There are exercises and spaces for journaling in the book. *Transitioning from Service* is simple and useful and I wish it had been published in time for my own transition. I suggest it to every transitioned or transitioning servicemember I speak with.

Soon after discovering Eric's book, I found Jason and Shauna's book, *Beyond the Military*. I just loved how Jason put into perspective what I was thinking and feeling. Jason introduces the reader to "fear-based energy" and how it guides many veterans toward bad decisions and life choices. He shares his educated thoughts on the "chemical withdrawal" of military transition. "In uniform we experience happiness as part of a band of brothers and sisters. Dopamine, oxytocin, serotonin and endorphins are released often, providing fulfillment and happiness in our warrior culture." Jason continues, "Our separation from the military culture removes us from the dealer that supplied and maintained our chemical addiction. Leaving the military disrupts our homeostasis and our bodies need to establish a new baseline in civilian society. Transition, therefore, requires a form of recovery." While I'm not a biochemist, I understood completely what he was describing. It made me more self-aware on my transition journey. Jason turns the all-familiar Military Decision Making Process (MDMP) into the Military Transition and Reintegration

Process (MTRP), giving the reader a logical step-by-step process to *take charge* of the transition, not the other way around.

Co-author Shauna Springer, PhD, closes out the book by taking the transitioning servicemember on a deep dive into forging healthy relationships. She introduces us to the evolution of battle-tested partnerships, a journey in the forming of trust between individuals, which ends with two individuals becoming lifelong battle buddies. She continues, "because of these relationships, you were at your best. You became something more. Secure attachment to those closest to us is the lifeblood of achieving our full potential. These attachments give us strength and clarity and when we lack this 'safe base' after transition, life can become chaotic."

What this made me realize was the difference between my relationships with other warriors compared to my relationships with businessmen and other non-veterans. It has made me keenly aware of the value of trust between me and those I interact with. Moreover, it has forced me to interact more, be more judicious in my selection of people and recreate the "safe base" I enjoyed in the military.

LOOKING BACK ...

I'll be the first to admit that taking care of my physical and emotional health during my military/civilian transition wasn't my highest priority at first, and that I made some missteps. Knowing what I know now, and looking back, here's what I've learned, with a few tips for you:

- In our years of service, we held sleep, diet and exercise in high regard even though we sacrificed some or all of them for the mission. In this encore life, you'll have better control over these (or at least you should). They will be no less important. I remember the Army's Performance Triad (Sleep, Diet and Exercise), created to keep soldiers at their peak. Along with my folded flag and retirement pin, I needed to carry the Triad with me into transition.

- Some of my friends have turned toward their religion. Great plan. Perhaps a renewed commitment to your faith is in order, with more involvement in your place of worship or with faith-based social and community activities. With greater control over your stability, you now have the ability to develop relationships in your faith group — or in your overall community — which can last and blossom.

- Communication with loved ones — friends, family, neighbors, colleagues — is essential in every step of your transition. Find military mentors who have traveled the path you are traveling (or about to travel) and connect with them often. Share your struggles, if for no other reason than to release the things that bother you. Find a new sergeant, a civilian mentor or mentors who can help "civilianize" you. Share your journey, let your guard down, explain your "well-worn paths" to them and let them be critical of you. Weekly I'm on a phone call or in person with another veteran sharing my frustrations and discoveries and hearing theirs. We both need that sounding board to convince ourselves we are not going crazy.

- It can be important to take a formal and deliberate approach to creating a "safe base" from which you can examine and approach relationships with the concentration of a fighter pilot. As Brené Brown states in her book, *Braving the Wilderness*, get up close and personal with folks very different from you. It's hard to misunderstand them when you do. I have found that refreshing and, more importantly, I've found that there are commonalities between us all — uniformed and civilian alike — like selflessness, loyalty and commitment to a cause. Your health and welfare cannot be an afterthought. I have not de-institutionalized yet, nor am I seeking to know when it will happen. I'm just doing the best I can to take care of myself and my family through it all. I am aware that there are more stressors ahead — more highs and lows and more transitions perhaps on the scale of what I experienced in 2016. This time, I'll be ready.

CONCLUSION

Making the leap from life in the military to life in the civilian world defies a simple description. It's magical, frustrating, easy, challenging, frightening, enlightening, difficult and amazing. The words you choose to describe the journey, and the path you choose to your encore life and career are up to you. As you embrace those choices and the possibilities before you, it is my hope that this book has informed the creation of your own path. You are now at the controls.

Rob with his new and only soldier, post-retirement: Duncan.

It is a newfound freedom I cannot overstate. I adore the Army but don't wake up these days with regret for deciding to retire from it. I value my ongoing connections with my military "tribe," but I don't feel a need to visit the VFW every night and tell war stories. I'm thankful for so much in this next life — this new life I'm living now.

I'm thankful for my institutionalization. It has helped me in this next journey, and I'll do my best to preserve the character, values and code the Army infused in me.

I'm thankful to have my Army wife, my trusty tribal member who understands who I am and what I'm going through better than anyone.

I'm thankful for my retirement pay.

I'm thankful for the time I am now afforded to take in the important stuff, my passions and my family.

I'm thankful to call myself a veteran.

. . . .

Your military experience has prepared you very well for this moment.

. . . .

Your military experience has prepared you very well for this moment. It has prepared you to analyze the decision, compare courses of action, then decide. It has prepared you to execute a thoughtful plan yet not fall in love with it. It has prepared you to maintain the flexibility to execute branch plans or contingencies as the environment and your situation changes.

Even amidst all these strengths, you can get your own transition wrong. I know this because of the mistakes I've made. Now immersed in a society I left behind in 1990, I'm very cautious not to take a pompous stand in front of those who have not served. I don't want to come off as out-of-touch or intending to make others feel unworthy. There are millions of people who never served in the armed forces, out there doing wonderful things inside their businesses and communities. They — like the best of the best in the military — are visionary leaders, courageous teammates and brilliant innovators. Alongside them, we can do so much.

What we bring into this next chapter — this encore life and career — is a large dose of what our nation needs. Many of us who have risked our lives and dedicated ourselves to a mission greater than ourselves are apt to look around

Robbie and Meggie's wedding party: the Campbells, Hamps and Rodmans (Alpbach, Austria, 2019).

in the civilian world and balk at political division, social unrest and unprofessional, inappropriate behavior (online and in person). It is because we conducted ourselves in our personal and professional lives to a higher standard ... for years and even for decades. The world can learn from us and we should continue to share all that we have been taught and all we have experienced. We might be but half of one percent of the U.S. population but our potential impact is tremendous.

Approach this transition as you did the most important missions you were assigned in the military. Dust off your pre-flight checklist, Ranger handbook, or military decision-making process. Put those troop-leading procedures into action. Your service will continue to serve you well.

PAY IT FORWARD

This transition should come full circle — as you learn from me and others, share what you've learned and experienced with the exiting servicemembers following in your footsteps. As you navigate each day, reach back to those about to exit the iron gates. Help them learn from you. One of our greatest gifts is that we understand each other as servicemembers on a level nearly impossible to explain. And, as I've highlighted, we are the small, few fish in a large pond. We ought to gather, "swim as a school" and lean on each other. I consider myself a mentor to several servicemembers who I've never met in person but who are on the cusp of what I experienced.

When I think about the formal assistance and "out-processing" offered by the Army to retiring lifers like me, I'm disappointed by the transition process and, sadly, I don't trust that it will improve greatly with age. That said, we can take charge of this — informally and as a powerful collective — by helping other veterans, their spouses and their families. Let's help them discover their true passion and help them travel an authentic path toward a passion-aligned job, entrepreneurship or a position on your team.

Even in the pause of a pandemic, the Campbell journey continues and I don't claim to have it all figured out. You won't either. By the time this book makes it to you, I cannot say for sure that I'll be in the same place doing the same thing. I know that I will grow and evolve, especially as the distance from my 2016 retirement grows. The Rob Campbell of 60 years will certainly be different from the freshly retired Rob Campbell of 50 years. I embrace this change and I'm excited to know the future me. My hope is that I remain true to my purpose and passions. My hope is that I can continue to enjoy the ride and take in the scenery. No door is closed, no path is blocked.

I'll close with this thought. Perhaps this transition journey is akin to driving at night. You can see as far as your headlights reach, but don't know what lies beyond them. You keep going anyway because you have faith — you chose a reliable, safe vehicle and a trusty co-pilot to take you there. You have options to pull off the road, change course or even stop and strategize before advancing.

That's the real beauty. It's on you. No more does the military get a say. Keep it authentic and keep driving, my friends. **The journey is remarkable, and the destinations are without limit.**

At ease.

PART THREE

PARTING THOUGHTS AND RESOURCES

Epilogue

WELL, WOULDN'T YOU JUST KNOW IT? EXPECT THE UNEXPECTED

President John F. Kennedy said, "When written in Chinese, the word crisis is composed of two characters — one represents danger, and the other represents opportunity." Now, in full disclosure, there has been some debate about the proper or improper translation of the word by the former President, but I need it for this epilogue ... so let's run with it, shall we? As I was placing the final touches on this book, my publisher Kate Colbert (who actually contracted COVID-19 but *soldiered* through it) suggested I write this last-minute addition to the book. As usual, she was right and I instantly felt duty-bound, amidst all that I had already shared with you, to write about the pandemic and its impact to my journey.

Less than four years into my re-entry into civilian life, the world shifted on its axis when an outbreak of a highly contagious respiratory virus — the 2019 novel coronavirus, SARS-CoV-2 or COVID-19 — became a global pandemic. Just as I was getting used to my "new normal," everything changed again. It was a crisis of epic proportion, full of danger *and* opportunity.

DANGER

The virus, the *black swan* of our times, closed businesses and gathering places, brought social distancing and stay-at-home directives, and challenged (and sometimes devastated) organizations and people in new, unexpected ways. Like everyone else, Leslie and I were overwhelmed by it all. I was in year three of my leadership business and year four of my new civilian life. I had gained several clients, was building a name for myself and began to expand my offerings with leadership speaking, coaching and teaching (all events that required the gathering of people). I had even hired an assistant. Of course, in my line of work, what I brought to businesses was an extra expense. I looked at it as an investment and still do, but I knew that when the going got rough, business leaders would be forced to make hard choices to conserve funds just to keep their businesses alive. For many businesses, an investment in Rob Campbell Leadership would not survive the cuts. Almost overnight, my business all but flatlined. I retained one client, a tech company whose business would survive the times. But there was little depth in my clientele and no assurances about the future. My cash on hand was good, thankfully, because I worked from home and had little overhead. I was grateful that we were OK but knew the business would only limp along until a *new normal* returned.

Leslie, an artist with her own art business and a rented studio across from our home, found herself in the same spot. As the virus gained momentum, I had joined her in Orquevaux, France, the first week of March, 2020, for a week of writing (book #3, and *At Ease* was already in the hands of my publisher and up for pre-order on Amazon). Leslie was in France on a two-month artist residency, in her element, interacting with other artists and carving out time for her own artistic growth. I returned home to Wilmington, North Carolina, on the 7th of March, 2020, and we decided the threat was not great enough for her to return with me. That all changed days later when the World Health Organization declared a global pandemic and our government issued new travel restrictions from Europe. We worried that if we hesitated, Leslie might be quarantined in France and unable to come home for an indefinite period of time. I scrambled to get her a flight and she returned home on the 13th. Not long after, we would find ourselves on a stay-at-home order in our apartment together, Leslie using our bedroom as a makeshift art studio while I worked from the living room. Like my leadership services, her art could be a short-term casualty as people tightened their purse strings to prepare for the unknown. Art is a luxury; so is business development. Our future was uncertain. (And, all the while, my book publisher, Kate, was adrift in the Atlantic Ocean on a cruise ship, blissfully unaware of the chaos that awaited her at home and the serious illness that was gunning for her.)

OPPORTUNITY

There was a humorous post on social media early in the crisis, which read:

> U.S. citizens: "They won't let us do anything or go anywhere!"

> U.S. military: "First time?"

Yup, we Vets have the crisis T-Shirt. Time for a branch plan! I was thankful for that. Leslie and I had been hardened by our decades serving. It not only made us more resilient to live amongst restriction, it also made us appreciate the danger.

I had been quietly pondering what opportunities existed in this time but it was again my pal Jim Hughes who asked it of me formally. I answered:

"Opportunity 1: This is a chance to update my business offerings to a shifting market." Like many of us combat veterans, I could offer the business world some assistance in crisis management and leadership from a "before, during and after" perspective.

"Opportunity 2: A chance to write about crisis." I cranked out a few articles that I then posted on LinkedIn and I crafted a new book proposal for book #3 (stay tuned!). Just a few weeks prior, in France, I had started what I assumed would be book #3 (a leadership book), but after the crisis gained steam, I shelved the manuscript, called it "future book #4" and drafted a proposal for a new book on crisis management and leadership. It's going to be fun to write and useful to organizations. We veterans do not play well with obstacles. We reduce them and go around or blow right through the middle. I used my remaining business funds on some innovative advertising and reached out to a few of my mentors for sage business advice.

. . . .

We veterans do not play well with obstacles. We reduce them and go around or blow right through the middle.

. . . .

Leslie didn't slow down either. Opportunity 1: The pandemic allowed her to create a few pieces specific to the times, such as "Heal," a painting of hands holding the earth and "Caution," a series for which Leslie repurposed some yellow caution tape into a few mixed media paintings. She also started a small but inspiring *#PutArtInYourYard* local movement following the hashtag she found on social media, hanging her art out for every passersby to see.

Opportunity 2 for Leslie came from the isolation and decreased distractions brought on by social distancing. Remember, she is an introvert ... so quiet, "alone time" is her happy place. Leveraging this, she dedicated time to research, exploring how to license some of her art.

Stuck at home, more people began to embrace communicating through virtual conferencing platforms like Zoom and Skype, so they could stay connected and do business while "social distancing." This brought about Opportunity 3 for Leslie. It opened some doors for her to connect with her artist network in different ways and compare notes about pandemic impacts to their creations. She'll move forward with that education and, like me, keep her foot on the gas pedal.

LOOKING BACK ... BUT THEN, LOOKING FORWARD

Damn right — looking forward! Recall the windshield versus the rearview advice? I need it too. Leslie and I learned a lot in these encore years and we believe they have readied us for this moment we are in. We've adopted a philosophy in our lives and businesses: "Show up" every day — through posting, creating, connecting, learning, writing and speaking. I am excited about the release of this book and I aim to take it on the road. It's surreal to imagine it in your hands, yet here it is. Our country will overcome this pandemic and military/civilian transition will resume. So will the sale of art.

Looking back, in light of the coronavirus pandemic and all it has done to change our lives, I'm thankful that we had already sold our house, downsized and serviced some debt. We pulled up the anchors that were holding us down, and that would have made navigating this crisis more difficult. Today, we have flexibility financially and geographically and that gives us both a new sense of peace.

In addition to my gratitude for the ability to weather this storm logistically and financially, I'm glad we stayed true to our passions. There is enough unhappiness during a crisis and the last thing either of us need is *self-inflicted* unhappiness. Life is disrupted and uncomfortable enough right now. Looking forward, we will be relocating into a larger apartment a few doors down, where Leslie will create another innovative space for a studio. Believe it or not, we'll save some money with the move and gain more space. We're looking forward to creating another nest, but we are aware that we'll get restless and ready for another big move even after that. We yearn for the mountains and will likely head that way at some point. Or not. Leslie and I retain the freedom and power to make that call, and it's liberating to know that such decisions will never again be made by the military or some company. Pandemic be damned, we can still see through the windshield, we have a reliable vehicle to take us there and we have each other. We shall endure. May you all stay safe and healthy.

ACKNOWLEDGMENTS

It takes a village or, in the case of this book, a city. This is the toughest portion of the book. You see, I've been guided, taught and loved by so many and I'm sure I'll leave out someone worthy of praise. First and always most important, my BFF in the whole world, high school sweetheart and the coolest chick on the planet, **my wife Leslie.** I'm only 50% a man and person without her. I'm so grateful to have had her by my side and often out in front — not only through an incredible 27 years serving our nation but in this encore life that we are navigating and embracing. Transition has been a period of profound change but the one constant, my enduring beacon, is my love and admiration of her.

To **my son Robbie and his wife, Meggie,** and **my son Louden,** who are all blazing their own paths in this world and making a difference. My love for them runs deep and I am proud to call myself their dad. To **my late father, Bruce M. Campbell**, my biggest fan and the epitome of a gentleman. He continues to inspire and influence me long after his passing. To **my in-laws, Conrad and Theresa Hamp,** who have supported and loved me and our family at every turn in this soldier's journey and beyond. To **my sweet Aunt Mary Campbell,** who passed away during the writing of this book; she is gone but leaves a great legacy in a loving family, selfless service to Plymouth State University and cherished memories my family and I treasure.

My "sis" Melissa, who is traveling her own journey with her husband and U.S. Navy veteran **Dominic**.

Gratitude to my "Council of Colonels" book review board: **Colonels (Retired) Scott Campbell** (my cousin!), **Suzanne Scott, Bill Butler, Tom Dorl, Pat Carpenter, Lieutenant Colonels (Retired) Brian Scott, John Fickel** and **Bill Raskin.** You'll experience a better book because of their sage advice and edits. To **Marva Campbell**, a dedicated U.S. Air Force spouse, who teamed up with her husband (my cousin) Scott to provide a "military family team" review of this book.

Lieutenant General Drew Poppas and my warrior brother **Colonel (Retired) Mark Edmonds**, career leaders and mentors of mine. LTG Poppas officiated my Army retirement with eloquence, making it such a treasured memory.

To my friends and mentors who got a sneak peek at the book and offered their gracious testimonials, **General (Retired) James T. Hill, Lieutenant General (Retired) Michael Ferriter, Colonel (Retired) Adam Rocke, U.S. Navy Captain (Retired) Scott "Topper" Farr, Former Army Captains Warren Lanigan, Pete Marston** and **Tim Kuppler.** To combat veterans, soldiers and rock star Military Spouses, **former Captain Marjorie Eastman** and **Specialist Siobhan Norris** and finally to combat veterans and authors **Chief Warrant Officer 3 (Retired) Robert "Bo" Brabo** and **Master Sergeant (Retired) Nathan Aguinaga.**

My amazing publisher, Kate Colbert, and her team at Silver Tree Publishing. Kate and her team took my infantryman-trampled and beaten manuscript and turned it into gold. I am so proud of this book and grateful to Team Silver Tree for every perfect touch, like the cover design and typesetting by **Courtney Hudson.**

A big thanks to **Jim Hughes, the Untamed Entrepreneur**. Jim is my life and business coach and dear friend, and is the only non-veteran associated with this book and he's the perfect fit. I've pursued my passions and chased my flow-state in large part because of Jim's influence on me. The book and my journey are incomplete without him, and his special contribution on the pages that follow is further evidence of his brilliance and generosity.

Major General (Retired) Mark Stammer, whose guidance and perspective on the cusp of my retirement decision was, as it always was, timely and just what I needed.

To **Colonels (Retired) Tim Scully and Jeff Martindale**, two soldiers who planted some needed seeds in my brain early in my transition, which set me on the right path.

Command Sergeant Major Kenny Wolfe, a friend and warrior who continues to give this old Colonel the dose of NCO perspective that he needs.

Ben Seegars, John Seegars and **Bobby Batchelor**, the leaders of Seegars Fence Company, my very first Rob Campbell Leadership client! **George Taylor, Adam Burke, David Reeser, Jerry Coleman, Shaun Olsen, Dallas Romanowski, Melissa Phillippi, Greg Ballard, Rich Novak and Nick Kovacic**, all smart, dedicated business leaders who opened their companies to me, who gave me a chance and taught me so much about private business and entrepreneurship. I'm proud to call them friends and mentors.

My VetToCEO brothers — **former U.S. Army Captain John Panaccione, U.S. Army Majors (Retired) Mike Horn** and **Taylor Mulkins,** and **U.S. Navy SEAL, SO1, Monty Heath** — selfless servers who taught me to be an entrepreneur. I feel like I'm back in the "rifle squad" when I'm with them. **Former U.S. Marine Sergeant Bill Kawczynski**, a tireless veteran servant at the University of

North Carolina, Wilmington, whose passion and commitment I strive to emulate.

Lieutenant General (Retired) Lawson Magruder and **Mr. Byrd Baggett of True Growth Leadership**, who helped me and so many others find their core purpose and live a life of authenticity.

Ziggy Attias and The Chateau Orquevaux Artist and Writer-In-Residence Program, Orquevaux, France, the birthplace of this book. **Marvin and Rebecca Knight**, whose farm we frequent when in Asheville, North Carolina. Books and paintings, not just vegetables, grow amazingly there because of their hospitality.

The Rock & Roll Hall of Fame band Radiohead deserves a special mention; I can write like a man possessed when those cats are playing!

The United States Army, who made this man a soldier, leader, and selfless servant. Second only to marrying my wife Leslie, my decision to join the Army remains my smartest.

Lastly, **to all the servicemembers, many of them my dear friends, who gave their lives for their country**. They will never live to see an encore life and career, but they will live forever in my heart.

Special Contribution by Jim Hughes

REACHING OUR POTENTIAL AND LIVING IN A STATE OF FULFILLMENT

*What follows is a meaningful overview of a proven framework
I learned from my entrepreneurial friend and mentor Jim Hughes,
who I first introduced you to in Chapter 4. Jim is the brilliant
and generous founder of Untamed Entrepreneurs. For me, practicing what Jim prescribed was surprisingly hard but real and
impactful. I needed this and I continue to need it. I think you,
too, may benefit from these veteran-specific insights and recommendations — which can save you from the distractors and
shiny objects that can take us off course. So it is with thanks to
Jim for penning this special section of my book that I turn you
over to his methodology and warmth, in his own words (and
British spellings!) ...*

Thank you for your kind and heartfelt introduction, Rob. I am immensely proud and flattered that a young British tosser like me can add value to a high performer and seasoned pipe swinger like yourself! Anyway, enough of the smoke blowing. Let's get into it, shall we?

Firstly, a brief introduction to me, why I do what I do and the value I hope to add through these words. My mission is to help people reach their potential and have fun, by aligning themselves and their work with who they truly are and what inspires them. This stems from a decision I made to find — and then live — my own purposeful life. A life truly aligned with my own identity, what I love to do, what inspires me and who I wish to serve. It is a journey that began three years ago and has taken me from a tired, demotivated and disillusioned employee, living a desk-based, 9-to-5 life in Australia to being a nomadic entrepreneur, traveling the world, engaging in my passions and running my perfect business as I go. Back then, as I lay in bed struggling to motivate myself to get up, the warning signs were there. Apathy was taking hold and the energy levels were dropping. I was no longer excited to get to work each morning and I understood what other people meant by "the Monday-morning blues." It had to stop. And so, the path to self-discovery, clarity and authenticity began.

I attended seminars and training all over the world, took online courses, read countless books, listened to hundreds of hours of podcasts, hired a mentor and picked the brains of anyone who would stay still long enough to hear me out. Finally, after more than 1,300 hours of my time and $25,000 I figured it out! Steve Jobs said it is "much easier connecting the dots looking backwards" and he was absolutely right. Once I reached this level of clarity, I realised — ironically — that my mission was to help people through exactly the same process I had been through ... except with much greater efficiency, accuracy and speed (oh, and a lot less money, of course!). The end result is a 6-Step Path that helps YOU reach your potential and have as much fun as possible on the way.

Steps 1 to 4 are what I call the Foundation Steps. It is these Foundation Steps I will be sharing with you in this chapter.

Before we dive into them, it's worth pointing out a couple of things:

- As with the rest of the advice in this book, this is not a prescription or a "how-to" manual. I am not in a position to suggest what kind of life or career you should create for yourself. What I can do, however, is ask you questions to promote introspection, invite you to question your old assumptions, and arm you with the tools and actions needed to figure this stuff out for yourself.

- Don't expect instant answers — this is not some kind of "life hack." Bamboo is the fastest growing plant in the world, helped by the fact it develops solid roots, long before it grows its shoots. Treat this like the root-growing phase and be patient ... it will pay off.

- There is no golden ticket. These questions and actions are just the beginning. A shit-load of work is required on your part once we're done here. Ready to go? Excellent.

THE 4 FOUNDATION STEPS

- **STEP 1:** "Now" — Where Are You Now?
- **STEP 2:** "You" — Know Yourself
- **STEP 3:** "Why" — Uncover Your Mission
- **STEP 4:** "Who" — Define Your Customer

STEP 1: "Now" — Where Are You Now?

Designing an epic life around who you truly are and what inspires you is a process — a journey of self-discovery and growth that will take you to previously unexplored places.

As you military lot know more than anybody, to navigate any journey, it helps to have a map. For a map to be useful, we need to know two things:

1. Where you're going, and

2. Where you are right now.

Step 1 is designed to figure out the second point — "where you are right now." By this I mean, how closely does your current role and life align with your true self, what you're best at and what inspires you? Are you surrounded by the people who support, encourage and challenge you? What does a perfect lifestyle look like?

These are just a few of the questions I suggest you ask yourself to find out where you are currently located, and, in doing so, to discover the distance you need to travel, and the rough direction you need to head in.

STEP 1 Actions

Giving each item below a score between 1 and 10 (with 10 being "most true" and 1 being "least true"), how true are each of the following statements?

☐ My environment is everything to me. The people I spend the most time with support, encourage and challenge me, taking me closer to reaching my goals.

☐ I know who I am. What inspires me, what I am best at and what I am weakest at.

☐ I know the mission and purpose of the company I work for, and it is aligned with my own.

☐ I know the customer I serve at work and am inspired to serve them.

☐ I have a clear vision for the future and a path to fulfill it.

Out of a possible 50 points, how did you score? Where might clarity be needed? If your score is low, fear not. The remainder of this chapter will help increase it.

STEP 2: "You" — Know Yourself

When we were young kids, we acted naturally. We had no filters or internalised guideposts as to how we were supposed to behave. We laughed when we felt like laughing, soiled ourselves when we felt like soiling ourselves and ran around naked, without a care as to how were being perceived. We were too young to define ourselves and we were conditioned to conform, so very quickly the opinions of others — particularly parents and teachers — became our reality. We didn't have to hear "Rob talks too much" many times to truly believe it.

To some extent, all of us still carry this adopted identity around. We wear it as if we created it: what we're good at, what we're crap at, how we should live our lives, how much money we should have and how much happiness we deserve. This becomes our "story," our narrative of who we are. What is under appreciated is that we will go to extraordinary lengths to remain true to this story. To not do so is to either be a liar or a hypocrite and, as a result, we will sacrifice our health, wealth, relationships and overall happiness in order to avoid this. The objective of this step is to separate your "story" from your "truth."

Do you know your story? Does it differ from the story other people have of you? If you were to ask five friends what you're best at, what would they say? What about things you're crap at or don't like doing? Do you have a true understanding of what these are? If you don't, I suggest you find out. I thought I was self-aware. I was confident that I knew what drove me, what scared me and where I added the most value. It was only when I decided I wanted to design my own business that I dug deeper into this area and realised how far off I actually was. I was framing some of my characteristics in completely the wrong way. What I perceived to be my biggest weaknesses were actually my biggest strengths. I was spending valuable energy trying to improve in areas I didn't enjoy so I could become someone I wasn't.

· ·

I was framing some of my characteristics in completely the wrong way. What I perceived to be my biggest weaknesses were actually my biggest strengths. I was spending valuable energy trying to improve in areas I didn't enjoy so I could become someone I wasn't.

· ·

How many of you judge yourself for not being good with details, instead of rewarding yourself for being a "big-picture thinker?" What about those of you who beat yourself up because you get bored easily? Have you ever considered that you thrive in fast-paced, ever-changing environments?

I bet most of you are guilty of this on some level — understandably so, in my opinion. The military is designed to cultivate good "all-rounders:" competent navigators, leaders, high-pressure decision makers, big-picture tacticians, detail-focused analysts, and of course lethal human weapons. The problem is that this broad range of skills, which is so highly valued when you're serving, may actually be the biggest obstacle on your path to clarifying your identity. How can you differentiate between a true passion and a learned skilled? Between a natural gift and something you have honed through hard work?

Unless you pay attention to some key indicators, it can be very tricky indeed. The longer your term of service, the deeper these dividing lines can be buried.

· ·

The military is designed to cultivate good "all-rounders:" competent navigators, leaders, high-pressure decision makers, big-picture tacticians, detail-focused analysts, and of course lethal human weapons. The problem is that this broad range of skills, which is so highly valued when you're serving, may actually be the biggest obstacle on your path to clarifying your identity. How can you differentiate between a true passion and a learned skilled?

· ·

A highly effective way of uncovering these lines is by identifying the times when you were in a state of flow. What do I mean by a state of flow? Have you ever heard top performers describe being "in the zone?" They talk of time slowing down — of mind and body in total harmony, a heightened state of awareness and of complete immersion in the task.

When we are "in flow," we are more energised, more successful and happier. If we are to truly reach our potential and live in a state of fulfillment, unlocking our own flow states will play a crucial role.

STEP 2 Actions

A tip before you start this exercise: Flow states can look different for everyone. You may have been in flow during combat, and I am in flow when skiing and when I'm coaching. For some, it's playing the guitar, for others, it's planning an operation. The more variety you can find in your flow state examples, the better.

Rob in a flow-state ... on his R1200GS BMW motorcycle.

1. Identify three to five occasions when you were in a state of flow. They can be work or social occasions, when you were younger or older, short lived or long lasting. Think long and hard. Even the most seemingly insignificant examples can be critical. Break each example down into the following criteria:

    a. *Environment*: What setting were you in?

    b. *Role*: What role were you playing?

    c. *Task*: What task were you performing?

    d. *Audience*: Who were you around? Who were you working with or for?

    e. *Impact*: What was your impact on those around you?

2. Assess your answers.
    - Are there any common characteristics throughout? *E.g., I am always in a team.*
    - Did anything crop up that you didn't expect? *E.g., I like brainstorming ideas.*
    - What are the key elements that would need to exist in your work or life to keep you in flow as often as possible? *E.g., I would need to be in an environment where I could create.*

- What other moments could you create that would induce a state of flow? *E.g., Surround myself with energising people and help them solve business problems.*

3. Create a list of what you presently regard as your biggest weaknesses. Then reframe each one as a strength. For example:

Perceived Weaknesses	Actual Strengths
• *Crap at details*	• *Great at seeing the big picture*
• *Never finish things*	• *Amazing at starting things*

STEP 3: "Why" — Uncover Your Mission

If you're unsure as to what I mean by your "why" or "mission," think of it as a purpose. An overarching life objective that is bigger and more significant than yourself. It is often defined by your passions, your gifts and your past. It is your North Star that will inspire you through the hard times, keep you focused in periods of distraction and provide a daily reminder of the potential impact of your efforts. For some, uncovering their purpose is easy; for most of us, however, it is not. Not all fulfilled people have a clear purpose, but all those with a clear purpose (that is being worked toward) are fulfilled.

. . . .

Not all fulfilled people have a clear purpose, but all those with a clear purpose (that is being worked toward) are fulfilled.

. . . .

Whether you're starting your own business or nailing down that perfect career move, the first step out of the military is the hardest. Stacking the deck in your favor is therefore a must if you want to succeed. Ever seen someone jump from one business idea to the next without ever getting any closer to success? What about those who rush from one corporate safety blanket to the next, choosing pay checks over passions? Do you think either example would exist if that person had a clearly defined purpose that inspired them on a daily basis?

If you have ever been in the position where you feel guilty for not being more motivated by what you're doing, you are not living your purpose. I sum it up like this: your purpose does not require MOTIVATION, it provides INSPIRATION. One is an energy drain, the other an energy source!

If what you're doing requires motivation, it is not aligned with your purpose! I spent ages trying to figure out my purpose. Prior to understanding what it was, I looked at numerous options for potential businesses. In every case, as soon as I realised the amount of work involved, I moved on — a surefire sign that these ideas were not aligned with my purpose.

So where might you uncover your mission or purpose? Let's get clear now ... this is easier for some than others. However, that does not mean you don't have one. Everyone does — you just have to look for it.

Our mission is so often linked to an experience or experiences we have been through. Something so impactful — in a positive or negative way — that it left an indelible mark on our thoughts, beliefs and actions.

STEP 3 Actions

1. List three to five **life-defining experiences** or moments. They can be:

    a. Major challenges you have overcome

    b. Life lessons you have learnt

    c. Epiphanies, realisations, wins or

d. Repeated patterns you have experienced over a sustained
period of time.

These life-defining experiences can be positive or negative experiences. Emotions you are desperate to help others either experience or avoid. For some, these moments are at the surface and therefore easy to pinpoint, but this is the exception and not the rule. You may have to dig quite deep to find yours!

For me, it was experiencing the cost of living and working out of alignment with who I truly am. I am therefore inspired to help others avoid the same experience and help them live their potential. What is it for you? Don't be afraid to jot down seemingly unimportant experiences that may have happened years ago. It can all help.

2. Let's go "7 Levels Deep"

I've always loved this simple, yet highly effective, set of questions designed to take you deeper than you have ever gone before, when figuring out why something is important to you. Find it at 7LevelsDeep.com.

Taking what you discovered in question 1, write down what you think your purpose or mission might be. Then on the line below, write down why this particular thing is important to you. Then on the third line, write down why the thing on the second line is important to you, and so on, until you have seven lines. Where did you end up? Somewhere unexpected, I bet. Let this settle for a while and see what else you discover. This may well be your mission in a nutshell!

_____

_____

_____

_____

_____

_____

_____

STEP 4: "Who" — Define Your Customer

If your mission determines WHAT overarching objective you want to serve, defining your customer determines WHO you want to serve. To clarify, defining your customer is not reserved only for entrepreneurs or business owners. In the military, you serve (and thereby add value to) a customer at some point in the chain, be it your own country, your unit, your superior officer or a foreign land you are defending.

Being inspired by who you are adding value to is just as important as being inspired by your overall mission. Not only will the inspiration keep you going through the hard times, but truly understanding your customer and being able to resonate with them on a deeper level is priceless if you ever interact with them directly. Why do you think so many veterans are inspired to help fellow veterans? What about single Mums (or should that be Moms)? How often do you hear of successful women on crusades to bring value to those navigating the same stormy seas? Too many entrepreneurs develop a great product but ultimately don't care about the person buying it. Too many career hunters fail to consider the end beneficiary of their labor. This creates a disconnection or apathy, which is hard to overcome. What do Johnny Cash, Oprah and Lady Gaga have in common? A strong resonance with their audience, born out of major life experiences.

. . . .

Too many entrepreneurs develop a great product but ultimately don't care about the person buying it.

. . . .

By the same token, customers are often put off by a service due to a lack of confidence that the service provider actually understands their needs. Don't get sucked into the "if I can make money, it's a good idea" trap. Get crystal clear on who you want to add value to and start serving them now. A good starting point would be to review STEP 3. Are there any characters who played a key role in your life lessons or significant experiences? Perhaps you would like to help people who are about to go through the same experience(s)? This is the case for me. My WHY is to help people align themselves with their purpose, passions and potential through entrepreneurship and my WHO are those about to embark on the same journey I undertook.

. . . .

Get crystal clear on who you want to add value to and start serving them now.

. . . .

Once you have pinpointed the demographic, it's time to get granular again ... really granular. Who is this person? What are their greatest needs? What characterises them? What are the emotional triggers with which you identify and resonate? What are they currently struggling with and how will you help them?

Create a specific profile (or avatar); give them a name, occupation and personality. The end result of this deep dive should be ONE specific profile with whom you completely relate and understand. The kind of person who, when you met them, you would have an instant bond. This process of tuning out the 99% to focus on the 1% is counter-intuitive but incredibly important. Of all the processes I have my clients go through, this is the one that meets the most resistance.

However, by getting over this initial hump and learning to love the idea of serving only "one client," you will set yourselves apart from the vast majority of other entrepreneurs or job hunters!

STEP 4 Actions

1) Look to your answers from STEP 3. Do any of those impactful life experiences point to you serving a particular person or demographic? Who do you resonate with the most and who resonates with you?

2) Think of who this person might be and what they might be like. Create a picture of this person in your mind and create a detailed profile of this person, including their name, age, salary, wants, needs, fears, challenges, etc. Don't be afraid to get creative.

By the end of this process you should have somebody in your mind who you understand fully and are deeply committed to helping in one way or another.

. . . .

And there we have it. The four foundational steps I believe are crucial if you are to design a life in alignment with who you truly are and what inspires you.

Throughout this book, Rob has done a great job of communicating how challenging the transition is, from the military institution — complete with guidelines, structure and support — to the outside world, where the next "main effort" is yours to decide, not handed to you in a briefing room.

The military did a great job taking away many of the basic uncertainties of life; questions such as "who do I call to fix my fence?" and "where shall we live next?" were answered for you. They did this to allow you to focus on the far more "significant uncertainties," such as staying alive and completing an operation in the most effective way.

As you transition to civvie street, these uncertainties will become reversed. Major life decisions are now in your hands (and your family's). The opportunities are endless. Unfortunately, so too are the distractions.

As Rob has pointed out, you won't be short of counsel. People will be desperate to help, and advice will come at you thick and fast. This chapter, and the book as a whole, was designed to help you know which advice to absorb, and which to dismiss. By leaning into these four steps — by digging deep and uncovering who *you truly are, what inspires you*, and *who you want to serve* — you will be equipped with the confidence and clarity needed to advance with purpose.

Remember this is YOUR journey, no one else's. Resist the temptation to pursue the path well-trodden, simply out of fear and scarcity. Do not be ruled by conventional wisdom. Yes, plenty of people have left the military before, but you are the *only person in the world* with your story, your gifts, your inspirations, your fears and your desires. This uniqueness is your key to an authentic life, and it is your responsibility to find it, hone it, and own it!

Your journey starts here. Now is the time to "Know Yourself and Find Your Playground."

Bravo Jim! In my own experience practicing what Jim prescribed, I found it hard but real. I was on the cusp of turning 50 and didn't feel I needed to conduct an elementary exercise to figure out my next path. Turns out I did need it and continue to need it. And it was anything but elementary. My happiness was on the table. Seek it or discard it for something fake. "Get your shit together, Campbell" (hearing the echoes of hardened leaders from my years in the infantry). My post-Army experience has been one of distractors and shiny objects, which call to me and take me off course. In the Army, I became very good at weeding out the distractors clouding my mission and vision focus. You could say this methodology was beat into me by numerous mentors who noticed my lack of focus and jerked me back on course. In the Army I was given my mission. In my new life, the mission was mine to create. I followed Jim's steps and discovered clarity but it alone was insufficient. It should be clear to you now why I made Jim one of my new mentors. He still is.

> In the Army I was given my mission. In my new life, the mission was mine to create.

Keep in touch with Jim and check out his resources just for veterans at TheUntamedEntrepreneur.com/Vets.

FURTHER READING AND RESOURCES

The space beyond your military/civilian transition date — beyond the gates of your last ship, base, fort, camp or barracks — is crowded with publications and organizations that are eager to help. There are many good ones but it's hard to know where to start. If someone wants to help you (or even to sell you a $20 book), do your research and get a sense of what their founding mission is. Determine if devoting your time, energy or money to a particular resource or program would really provide value to you. Some claim to understand today's servicemember but many fall short. Many are just hyper-focused on translating military occupational skills, resume building and job placement but they overlook your *why*.

To help you navigate the sea of opportunity and voices, here is a collection of readings, websites and videos you may not know to look for. I have personally read these books, visited these websites, watched the videos and/or attended their programs.

1. ***What Color is Your Parachute? A Practical Manual for Job-Hunters and Career-Changers* by Richard N. Bolles.**
   A handful of great exercises you can complete to help you

determine what it is you really want to do. But start with your *why*! This book is updated frequently.

2. ***The 4-Hour Work Week: Escape 9-5, Live Anywhere, and Join the New Rich* by Timothy Ferriss.** An entertaining and useful book, which turns work and the workweek on its head. Tim's timesaving and passion-seeking methods are refreshing and inspiring.

3. ***Rich Dad, Poor Dad: What the Rich Teach Their Kids About Money That the Poor and Middle Class Do Not* by Robert T. Kiyosaki.** A good money philosophy for your changing financial situation.

4. ***Big Magic: Creative Living Beyond Fear* by Elizabeth Gilbert.** Excellent for those of us who want to tap into our creative side after service. A great perspective and real motivator.

5. ***Tribe: On Homecoming and Belonging* by Sebastian Junger.** This will put much of what you are feeling and will experience into perspective. It helped me realize I was not going insane.

6. ***It's Personal, Not Personnel: Leadership Lessons for the Battlefield and the Boardroom* by Colonel Rob Campbell.** Selfish plug. As a veteran, you will probably enjoy the whole book but Chapters 5 and 6 focus on self-awareness and introspection, which are essential as you transition.

7. ***Separating from Service: The Mental Health Handbook for Transitioning Veterans* by Eric Burleson (former Green Beret).** Great perspective on losing your identity yet maintaining your health. Easy but impactful read. Great exercises for you and your partner.

8. ***Beyond the Military: A Leader's Handbook for Warrior Reintegration* by Jason Roncoroni and Shauna Springer, PhD.**

Excellent book, which introduces the "Military Transition and Reintegration Process" or MTRP. Great exercises and clarity of what you are feeling. I emptied a highlighter on this book.

9. ***Braving the Wilderness: The Quest for True Belonging and the Courage to Stand Alone* by Brené Brown.** Excellent primer for interacting with strangers. Excellent book for entering the polarized world we currently live in.

10. **TheUntamedEntrepreneur.com/Vets** – Find Jim Hughes here! When I coach transitioning veterans, Jim is at the top of my mind. I've connected numerous Vets to Jim and they are living better lives because of it. Including me!

11. **TrueGrowthLeadership.com/Our-Services/True-Growth-Online-Seminar** –True Growth Online Academy. While the in-person seminar is best, this short, web-based program will help you zero in on your core purpose. You can find their book, *True Growth: Simple Insights on How to Live and Lead with Authenticity* by the LWM III Consulting Solutions, on this site.

12. **VetToCEO.org** – For those considering being their own boss, being an entrepreneur. Fantastic 7-week course run by seasoned entrepreneurs with decades of experience (not young veterans who claim to be entrepreneurs but are really not). I'm VetToCEO's Executive Director only because I believe it to be the very best.

13. **RobCampbellLeadership.com/Book** – This specific link, found in my 1st book, is where you can find self-awareness personality tests, my BIO Sketch and steps to create your own BIO Sketch. All essential as you start your journey.

14. **YouTube.com/watch?v=LBvHI1awWaI** – TEDx Talk, "Why Comfort Will Ruin Your Life" by Bill Eckstrom. Excellent perspective on where real growth actually occurs. You'll

resonate with his words, given your military service, but can apply it to your encore life. Assess where you stand at: ECSellInstitute.com/Bill-Eckstrom-The-Growth-Rings.

15. **YouTube.com/watch?v=9XRPbFIN4lk** – TEDx Talk, "Sell your crap. Pay your debt. Do what you love." by Adam Baker. This young speaker did his homework and delivers a thoughtful message. It spoke to Leslie and me both. Worth a watch.

16. **Ted.com/Talks/Doris_Kearns_Goodwin_Lessons_From_Past_Presidents** – TED Talk, "Lessons from Past Presidents," by Doris Kearns. Striking an inner balance between work, love and play. Powerful and just right for embarking on the next chapter.

GO BEYOND THE BOOK
KEEP IN TOUCH WITH ROB (AND LESLIE) CAMPBELL

FIRST THINGS FIRST. KEEP IN TOUCH!

You can find Rob hanging out and making a difference
in a few places.:

- 🌐 **RobCampbellLeadership.com** – An evolving and relevant
  site where you'll find videos of Rob speaking about leadership
  and veteran's issues. Or visit his blog page for frequent, useful
  content. Here you can find his books or just stay in touch!

- 💼 **LinkedIn.com/in/RobCampbellLeadership** – Rob is there
  daily posting, responding and sharing useful content on leadership, crisis management, and veteran and military spouse transition issues and entrepreneurship.

- 🌐 **VetToCEO.org** – A 501(c)(3) Non-Profit Veteran Entrepreneurship Program. Come join the cause! VetToCEO is one of
  Rob's post-military tribes, a group of seasoned and selfless
  veteran entrepreneurs countering traditional narratives and
  working hard to reduce the obstacles veterans encounter when
  seeking to enjoy their new freedom.

- 📘 **Facebook.com/RobCampbellLeadership** – That's right, he
  is there … Better late than never. Send him a message, a friend
  request or follow.

Curious to see artist Leslie Campbell's gatherings and creations, and learn more about her encore life and career? Visit her website at RavenWorks-Studio.com or connect with her on Instagram at @ravenworks_studio.

NOW, HOW TO DEEPEN THE RELATIONSHIP AND LEARN MORE? GO BEYOND THE BOOK.

Hire Rob to:

- **Speak and Inspire**. Rob speaks and inspires audiences on a variety of leadership and veteran and spouse advocacy topics.

- **Get Your Organization Ready to Hire Vets**. Rob can train and prepare your organization to be "Veteran Ready" — to recruit, hire, onboard and retain America's transitioning warriors and their amazing spouses.

- **Deliver Impactful Leadership Training.** Rob can train your leaders on contemporary leadership approaches for today's volatile, complex and increasingly virtual business environment.

- **Coach You or Your Colleagues to Success**. Rob coaches leaders and veterans on their leadership or transition journeys.

- **Prepare You for the Realities of Crisis Management and Leadership.** Rob can help you understand how to lead before, during and after crisis. With deep expertise in leadership and management under chaos and drastic change, Rob can bring strategy, calm and compassion to organizations turned upside down.

Get the conversation started at Rob@RobCampbellLeadership.com.

ABOUT THE AUTHOR

Colonel Rob Campbell (USA, Retired) entered the Army in 1990 and served a 27-year career as an infantry officer, ranger and paratrooper, commanding infantry and cavalry units from platoon to brigade. Rob is a veteran of the wars in Iraq and Afghanistan, with service in the 25th Infantry Division and the 82nd and 101st Airborne Divisions. He also served during Hurricane Katrina relief efforts in New Orleans, Louisiana. Rob's core purpose in life is to make a difference in the lives of others through optimistic leadership. Clear on this purpose, Rob decided to retire from the Army in 2016 and continue to give back to the community at large.

Rob wrote his first book, *It's Personal, Not Personnel: Leadership Lessons for the Battlefield and the Boardroom*, in 2017 and became an entrepreneur, founding a leadership coaching, speaking and consulting business. Rob is a staunch supporter of veterans and their spouses. He serves as the Vice President for the Association of the United States Army, University of North Carolina, Wilmington sub-chapter. He is also the Executive Director for VetToCEO, a 501(c)(3) non-profit veteran entrepreneurship program and an advisor to the MILSPO project, supporting military spouses.

Rob shares his leadership lessons on stage in front of businesses and government organizations, coaching business executives and training leaders. He enjoys adventure motorcycle riding, travel, reading and writing.

Rob is a native of Massachusetts and graduated from the Massachusetts College of Liberal Arts in North Adams, Massachusetts. He has Master's degrees from Central Michigan University and the United States Army War College. Rob is married to the former Leslie Ann Hamp. He and Leslie have two sons, Robbie and Louden. Rob and his wife Leslie settled on the North Carolina coast. *At Ease* is Rob Campbell's second book.

Ready to evolve your leadership skills with people-centric leadership lessons from a fellow veteran who, like you, has "been there and done that?" Pick up your copy of *It's Personal, Not Personnel!*

Before there was *At Ease*, there was *It's Personal, Not Personnel: Leadership Lessons for the Battlefield and the Boardroom*. There has never been a more important time — in corporate America and in the American military — for leaders, at all levels, to understand how to invest in people. In his first book, for a broad audience of leaders in every environment, Rob Campbell offers true stories and practical frameworks you can easily apply. But understanding that leadership is personal, you will begin to understand that all workplace challenges — productivity issues, efficiency issues, turnover problems, lack of employee engagement —all come down to whether employees are being acknowledged, valued and understood.

Available on Amazon in paperback, Kindle and audiobook editions.

Made in the USA
Columbia, SC
17 May 2020